Initiating
And I
Gene
Change

Entry and Contracting For Emergent Outcomes In Results Driven Organizations

TOVA AVERBUCH

BMI Publishing
Bushe-Marshak Institute for Dialogic Organization Development
3898 Trenton Place
North Vancouver, BC
Canada V7R 3G5
info@B-M-Institute.com

Library and Archives Canada Cataloguing in Publication
Title: Initiating and inviting generative change: entry and contracting for emergent outcomes in result driven organizations / by Tova Averbuch.
Names: Averbuch, Tova, author.
Description: Series statement: BMI series in dialogic organization development; 7 | Includes bibliographical references.
Identifiers: Canadiana 2021027798X | ISBN 9781777184643 (softcover)
Subjects: LCSH: Organizational change. | LCSH: Organizational learning.
Classification: LCC HD58.8.A94 2021 | DDC 658.4/06—dc23

Imprint: BMI Publishing

Page design: Vancouver Desktop Publishing Centre
Illustrations by Aliza Fruchtman

Dedication

To the infinite process of coming into being

To my late mother, Dr. Nehama Röza-Goldman, for genuinely sharing her bountiful "head bubble"—my favorite way of learning.

To my late father, Yossef Goldman, for silently sharing his craftsmanship and humor—my favorite ways of making inner spaces.

To my late husband, Dr. Mickey Averbuch, for teaching me profound humility.

Most of all to my children, Assaf and Shira Averbuch, for learning together the joy of life, love and play we share.

Gratitude and Acknowledgements

I would like to express my appreciation and gratitude to those without whom this book would not have come to light: to Gervase Bushe for your invitation, trust and support to write this book and for the joy of co-creating. To Bob Marshak for evoking more conceptualization in this book. To Peggy Holman for provoking and encouraging my professional writing in English, coaching me into this writing, and for your precious friendship. To Aliza Fruchtman for the gift and joy of co-creation and for your masterful illustrations that are bringing new life to the Swirling Spiral Model.

I am happy to acknowledge a few of my teachers, thinkers and practitioners, who changed me and my work: To Edgar Schein for adding heart, imagination and deep symbolic thinking into professional OD work from the start. Special thanks and gratitude for our conversation, provoking and evoking my thinking about dialogic roots as they reflect in my work today. To David Bohm for the gift of dialogue and opening my eye to deep listening as a social revolution. To Harrison Owen for a new world of being and doing that pushed up the ceiling for me to see sky. Thank you for Open Space Technology and for your mentoring and friendship along the way. To Angeles Arrien for being my guide to become a better and fuller person-professional as a way of life. To Eugene Gendlin for the gift of working with my felt sense to invite deeper authenticity and life flow. And to Otto Scharmer for finding ways to talk of and from spirit in business organizations, leading from the future as it emerges.

To my companions in the infinite game of living: my dear sister, Hava Barouch, and my best friends—you know who you are—who supported me and helped in many ways to make this writing possible.

A whole hearted gratitude to my colleagues, my clients and my students, for being road companions to this infinite game of experimenting, learning and becoming.

This book is the fruit of our walking together.

Contents

Foreword by the Series Editors

The term *Dialogic Organization Development* was first used in a 2009 article we published in *The Journal of Applied Behavioral Science.* In that article, we described how organization development had evolved and contrasted it with the original form of OD, which we labeled Diagnostic OD. We were unhappy with how OD textbooks continued to treat the newer premises and practices as if they fit the earlier model. We wanted to create a space for people to think about, research, develop, and discuss these newer approaches to change. This book series is a continuation of that ambition and purpose.

Dialogic OD is a still-developing mindset (rather than a set of specific methods). It is rooted in two key intellectual movements that influence all social sciences: how social reality is constructed, maintained, and changed by how we talk (post-modernism) and how social systems emerge and self-organize without leadership direction or a plan (complexity science). We have written several articles and book chapters about this, and readers of this book (and all books in the series) are encouraged to access our website, www. B-M-Institute.com. Most of our writings and those of some others are available there for free. The articles and book chapters on the website provide a general overview of Dialogic OD theory, how it is the same and different from Diagnostic OD, and basic ideas about leadership, consulting, change, and creating great organizations embedded in Dialogic OD.

Since 2005 we have devoted time and attention to conceptualizing and explaining Dialogic OD. Now we turn our focus to encourage presentations of specific dialogic practices applicable to all change methods and approaches. Each book in this series is a short, focused, and practical exploration of one topic to expand the theory and practice of Dialogic OD. We hope you enjoy the books. We welcome proposals for further volumes.

If you are relatively new to this set of ideas, you can download and read the free "Companion Booklet to the BMI Series in OD" by visiting www.b-m-institute.com website.

Gervase R. Bushe
Robert J. Marshak
October 2019

Introduction

"Out beyond ideas of wrongdoing and rightdoing there is a field, I will meet you there" (Rumi)

If you are a Dialogic organization development practitioner and leader, or consider practicing the dialogic way, and you find yourself asking the following questions:

- What needs to be done differently, from the start, if I want to work dialogically?
- How can I avoid falling back onto the well paved roads of the knowing, expert stance?
- How can I smoothly negotiate and contract from a dialogic, 'not knowing' stance, with results-driven individuals?

This book can guide your entry process by helping you understand what is needed and why throughout the entry and contracting stages of a generative dialogic process. It is my theory of practices for how to prepare leaders and members to successfully engage in a dialogic and emergent process aimed at addressing a complex problem with seemingly no easy answers.

This book offers ways you can be, think and do dialogic work as a person and an organization development practitioner. This dialogic and emergent way is reflected in three ways: many stories from my personal practice of using dialogic processes in various organizational systems, descriptions of actual step by step guidance for action, and in the conceptual working model and underpinnings of my Dialogic OD work.

For 45 years I have worked as an external organization development (OD) consultant. In the last 25 I have primarily worked with dialogic large group methodologies, from a dialogic mindset (Bushe & Marshak, 2015). My practice is mainly in large scale whole system process interventions in situations of confusion when leaders are seeking an answer to a complex burning issue. (Comment: when I use the same mindset, skills, theory and principles in limited scale it works effectively as well). Most of my work is done within limited time frame of 3-6 months. My clients are high tech industry, government, military, communities and cross sector initiatives at local, national and international level. My experience has taught me that dialogic processes can be valuable and fruitful in any situation where people are facing a real burning issue with multiple stakeholders and have no simple answer. Working with the whole system in a limited/short time span on a burning issue is an intensifier and accelerator of the process.

If ever we needed proof that life is becoming more and more unpredictable; more Volatile, Uncertain, Complex and Ambiguous (VUCA), the COVID-19 pandemic and the turbulence it brought into the world has turned this idea into visceral knowing. It seems we are all in a never-ending beginning—as soon as you feel you have a grip on the story, you are back to stage one. Major changes, turbulence and disruptions have become the new normal. Nothing we did before prepares us sufficiently to know what to do next.

When we meet complex situations, situations in which we are unable to see any pattern of cause and effect (Snowden & Boone, 2007), our first tendency is to simplify or to familiarize the unfamiliar by saying, "this looks exactly like something I know", to gain some ability to make sense of the situation. Without a coherent story line, complex situations are often narrowed down into a bi-polar story line: good or bad; for or against, either/or. By narrowing the perception of complexity, we calm our anxiety and get a false sense of control. The cost is—inadequate inquiry and ineffective solutions.

When a disrupted and complex situation meets performance-based, and results-driven leaders and organizations, Dialogic OD offers effective processes to meet uncertainty and navigate complexity. With a dialogic mindset we look at reality knowing we do not know. We use collective processes to orient ourselves and make meaning as we go along, while tolerating the not knowing and the never- ending beginnings of stepping with purpose into the always unfolding unknown (Shaw, 2002).

Why Beginnings?

Birth and beginnings hold the full potential of what's to come, so some essential qualities must be present from the beginning.

This book focuses on getting started, initiating, because of the critical importance of beginnings in general and in dialogic, emergent, work processes in particular. Beginnings are essential to Dialogic OD both as formative initial stages of the work, and as a fresh, curious and open state of mind—beginner's mind.

The initial stages of entering and contracting are usually perceived by consultants as "pre-work"; necessary and critical components, but not really part of the professional assignment. I hold the stance that any interaction we have with the client is an intervention. From the first hello to walking together to a meeting, the process of exploring, contracting—all. There is no pre-work. It is all interventions. In this book I will show how entering, contracting and readiness assessment are a critical and vital component in our professional work. They are the conception and birthplace of dialogic relations, climate, mindset and process. Everything has a beginning. Complexity research shows us that initial actions, beginnings, are fateful. As most of my practice is short term engagement, initial steps become even more critical because of the timeframe.

Our responsibility as consultants is to embody our dialogic mindset authentically in who we are as people and how we conduct ourselves as practitioners in the beginning and throughout the dialogic process. To succeed in transformative change, essential characteristics of dialogue must be present from the beginning of our relationship with the client in our presence, conduct, process-design and contracting. By starting a consulting process in a dialogically embodied way, your client system experiences the distinct dialogic presence and mindset of Dialogic OD in every interaction. Being a dialogic person-professional helps generate trust and intimacy in all relationships, preparing our clients for the work to come. From their relationship with us, clients learn viscerally by directly experiencing a dialogic mindset and emergent process, rather than hearing and being taught about it. There is never enough time to teach all that is needed before you intervene. The more you manifest it, the less 'preaching and objections' you encounter. It's easier for clients to learn as we walk along.

What is in the book?

This book presents an elaborated dialogic mode of being and doing through the formative stages of the change process. It is for anyone seeking to bring life, generativity, engagement and joy to people and organizations; to navigate complexity, and to bring creativity and vitality to any human system.

This book is designed for **new and experienced OD practitioners** who:

- Find the initial stages of dialogic OD challenging and would like some guidance and deeper understanding on forming dialogic relationships with internal and external potential clients.
- Find it awkward to insist on essential conditions for genuine Dialogic OD process.

And for **leaders** who:

- Are sick and tired of hierarchal and linear ways.
- Doubt the suitability of 'expert models' of knowing in virgin territories.

The **first part** of the book is dedicated to the practical theory that informs and communicates the thinking about the practice:

Chapter 1 lays out the theoretical ground I am building on explaining when and why Dialogic OD process is useful, and how to work with the innate paradox of offering emergent process to result driven organizations.

Chapter 2 offers a working model, 'the swirling spiral model', which gives shape and name to the underpinnings of emergent, dialogic work. It lays out the sequence of widening circles of entering and engaging with the client system (spiral) and the energetic flow from authentic presence in beginner's mind to emergent outcomes in each one of the circles (swirl). Each entering circle resolves its main task and enables going up the spiral to another beginning that engages a larger group of people.

In Chapter 3 I describe why beginnings are so important in every process and how they are tied to emergence, generativity, and narrative, both as formative stages but also as a beginner's state of mind. In this chapter you will also learn about the unique nature of outcomes and endings in emergent processes.

The second part of the book presents the practice, step by step guidance for creating conditions for success, inviting vital interaction and evoking creative energy. These chapters are supported by stories from my practice, to illustrate how it actually happens.

Chapter 4, on readiness, refers to the pre-formal contracting phase of our work with the client. Here I describe what you need to know and how to engage with the client so that you both can discern the suitability of dialogic process to the issue presented, to the client and to yourself.

Chapter 5 walks you through the process of aligning with the Caller, the person who sees the need and connects us with the organization, and partnering with the sponsor, the authority in charge, accountable for the issue we are called to assist with. Since, in complex situations, the sponsor is the person(s) you are journeying with, looking for a path to generate transformation, special emphasis is made on creating a covenant relationship, not only a transactional partnership of joint interests, with the sponsor.

Chapter 6 is a comprehensive guide for contracting for Dialogic OD work, which gives special attention to doing it in a way consistent with the principles and practices of Dialogic OD. Contracting this way is uncommon to most people. Many find it challenging to establish both a formal contract and a psychological contract needed for successfully stepping into a generative change process, where the actual process is to be chosen together and the outcomes are unknown.

Chapter 7 concludes the practice part of the book by describing two more entry points for widening circles of engagement: the management team and a diverse stakeholders' planning team. This chapter reminds you to work with management keeping in mind that in most cases they are not used to dialogic and generative engagement of stakeholders.

It describes the steering committee/planning team formation as a microcosm of those diverse stakeholders, and how they lead, co-operate, co-create and co-own the emergent, generative change process.

A concluding note offers how to start right away.

One last personal note about beginnings: as an emigrant to Israel at the age of four, I have been fascinated with beginnings all my life. The concern and worry of what and how will it be and become... the fresh smell of infinite possibilities...the whoosh of adrenalin coupled with the sweet sense of adventure... Yes, I am afraid. Yes, I feel vulnerable and exposed, but YES, I feel so alive and pregnant with potential! I know that not all of us love beginnings, I know none of us loves it all the time. But all of us meet them every day. Befriending beginnings can be beneficial as they are becoming more and more our prominent reality.

Writing this book was an emergent dialogic process. Dialogue between me and my practice, reality and conceptualization and with people (most of them I acknowledge in the beginning of the book) who disrupted or challenged my habitual way of thinking and expressing myself. Sometimes it was pleasant and other times not so much, yet it was always extremely valuable in keeping the process of writing alive and emergent, feeding my search towards a fuller and more truthful integration.

I hope you find your experience with the book usefully disruptive and joyful.

PART ONE
Practical Theory

"In the beginner's mind there are many possibilities, but in the expert's mind there are few"

—*Shunaryu Suzuki*

ONE

Dialogic OD Work in Organizations

Assuming that most leaders in organizations are results-driven and tend to have controlling leadership habits, how do you contract for self-organization and emergence? Supposing managers and workers are primarily evaluated according to their personal contribution to known and preplanned measurable results:

- Why and when is it conducive to start down a path without specific predetermined outcomes?

Why and When?

I begin with a story about a company facing a global dot-com industry crisis with whom I worked for about three months. It illustrates both why we need to contract for emergent outcomes and when Dialogic OD can be beneficial (Averbuch, 2015).

INN, a communication-infrastructure company, selling to governments all over the world, was in crisis. INN was in its third round of layoffs and was desperate for cash. Harriet was a trusted managerial consultant working there. She was asked for a name of a creative marketing specialist to help INN sell more ASAP. Harriet realized that internal alignment, not marketing, would be a better strategy in a dead market. When an opportunity presented, they would be ready and first to respond. Harriet suggested hiring me.

I met with management (and Harriet), learned their struggles and desires. The issue at hand was INN's survival. We created a diverse planning team of people who answered the call to design a process to address the question "How do we make One Million Dollars in this coming year?" Harriet and I co-facilitated the event.

> One hundred and forty people responded to an invitation to a dialogic event and worked for two days and a night. It was right before the fourth round of layoffs in which 100 of the remaining 420 employees had to go. While painful, those gathered decided to help this organization stay alive not knowing who would be laid off tomorrow. Using Open Space Technology (Owen, 1997), people created an agenda for two days during the first hour. Everyone had a voice. There was a palpable sense of community pride. By the end of the second day, implementation groups formed to detect and address misalignment issues all over the organization and other initiatives that people believed to be helpful. The organization came to life as a community to revive the business. From this stage on I was not in contact with the organization (that was our contract from the start). All that emerged in the gathering was used and assimilated into the organization independently. Harriet continued to be their management consultant and all that is written next is from her perspective.
>
> Over the next six months, they tried to sell their products with no immediate success—country-wide infrastructure projects usually take a full twelve months for a sale to mature. Still, meaningful results, such as better alignment, cohesiveness, and energy level in a difficult struggle had resulted in a determination not to give up. The cohesiveness of this large group of employees enabled the owners to negotiate selling the firm as "one working enterprise" and not in bits and pieces. Eleven months after our gathering the remaining 320 employees were bought by another firm. A month after the acquisition, the acquiring company's stock price rose dramatically; a major sale of INN communication infrastructures, started one year ago, materialized that month.

This story exemplifies both when and why to contract for Dialogic OD. The first part illustrates one of the most appropriate examples of **when** to use Dialogic OD: in complex situations of crisis and uncertainty when the system faces a sense of not knowing what to do about a burning issue. An invitation to partake in a real burning issue, to which there is no straightforward answer, tends to draw people in. Working for their shared intention/purpose while using emergent processes encourages self-organization, evokes collective meaning-making and wise action.

In the second part of the story, we witness **why** we need Dialogic OD processes, especially in complex situations of crisis and uncertainty. Unforeseen possibilities emerge when people choose to care, dare to engage in conversation, and take responsibility for creating a viable future for each and all, not delegating it to an expert or a leader. The whole system saved both people's jobs and the business activity, allowing considerable gain for shareholders. These outcomes could not be planned or led—"top-down"—according to premeditated targets and milestones.

Theoretical roots

Though this book aims to make practice accessible, I find it important to briefly present some of the relevant theoratical roots I am workiing from.

Dialogue

Martin Buber (1970, first published in 1923) made the proposition that humans find their meaning and growth through relationships and address existance in two ways :"I–it", addressing others as objects, separate, limitted, as if their only function is to get us what we want. The other possibility is "I–thou", addressing others in relationship where we see their full humanity and bring our full humanity in reciprocity and mutuality. All moments of growing and becoming need a 'thou' to happen. Dialogue is a **'whole person'**, personal and engaged way of relating. We live an exsistental stuggle day in and day out between these two ways of relating. For me this is the ground of OD in organizations: striving for "I-thou" relationships and moments in every social context.

David Bohm (1996) proposed dialogue as a way of exploring reality, the collective seamless whole, through process. It is done by paying attention to the personal and collective thought process, not to the content. This proposition grounds me in the practice of staying open, curious, and suspending judgment while listening and observing. It helps me be an engaged yet, at the same time, reflective participant in the '**whole system'** I am part of as a member and/or a facilitator. I see Edgar Schein's contributions, especially **process consultation and humble inquiry** (1988, 2021), as ground breaking adaptations of these two dialogic forms—combined with sociological theories—to the organizational field.

I want to propose that all dialogue forms mentioned here have three intentions in common:

- To expand consciousness, personal and collective.
- To cultivate intimate human relationships

and by doing so:

- To make the world a better place

These dialogic practices are not intended to converge into immediate collective decision making or action, even though the quality of decision making and action is bound to improve when wider consciousness and human relationships evolve. These dialogic practices are mostly practiced in dyads, small and medium size groups.

I believe Dialogic OD shares the above humanistic intentions of dialogue and is deeply rooted in dialogue yet works with it a bit differently—as a pragmatic means to address complex situations when a practical answer is urgently needed. Dialogic mindset and methodologies are seen as a suitable, sometimes inevitable, modus operandi in situations that a simple answer cannot resolve. Dialogic OD shifts the focus from the individual to the interactions. Focusing on structuring the interactions, rather than taking the time to develop individual skills and perceptions in every person, makes it possible to implement Dialogic OD in larger scale and shorter time. Though I am convinced that the Dialogic OD practitioner ought to be dialogic in their consciousness and relational skills, the participants in the process do not. They just need to show up willing to bring their best effort to the task.

Dialogic OD as a way of changing systems can start with urgent needs to be dealt with, or can start from an aspiration to change an organizational culture. I usually work short term with systems in urgent need. I find that real urgent needs are a great starting point. Full of life and pregnant with potential. Operating from the belief that everything we do with the client is an intervention, and working dialogically from the very beginning, helps create aligned and innovative results quickly, expand consciousness and humanize relationships. First you do and then you listen and learn. Sometimes the process is taken further to become an organizational culture, a way of life. If not, it is often registered in people's memory as an alternative way to be and do when the waters get rough, or they feel stuck while facing a complex situation. Both have their value.

Differentiation and Integration (D/I) Theory

Originating in Biology, differentiation and integration theory is also used in organization and community work. The understanding that systems, social systems included, develop through ongoing differentiation and integration process (Janoff, 2021) is fundamental to emergent dialogic processes. In differentiation we mean inviting the whole person, and all diverse voices in, while listening to differences. In integration we mean letting all the different perspectives emerge into a new integrated understanding and fabric of relationships, ideas and actions (Weisbord and Janoff, 2000). As human beings we prefer the comfort of similarities yet need the diversity to be generative. Staying in listening when we are frustrated and feel attacked by other people's perspectives takes effort and sometimes courage but is inevitable as a practice, at least some of the time, for large and complex systems to evolve.

D/I theory takes place in many ways. Future Search is a methodology (Weisbord and Janoff, 2000) that makes an intentional effort to dance between homogeneous to heterogeneous group structures activating the D/I process in search of wider and more profound integration.

CONTEXT: what is the organization facing that led them to seek help?

Context is my first and last guide in sensing and assessing the suitability of a Dialogic OD process. The specific instance, the specific occurrence of the problem (Gendlin, 2007) is my gateway to knowing what is needed next. When assessing the context, bear in mind that Dialogic OD is appropriate under the following conditions:

Urgency: There is a burning issue that people care about that cannot be resolved simply.

Complexity: They are dealing with an adaptive challenge to which a known technical solution will not answer (Heifetz & Laurie, 1997). A situation with no predictable patterns, no predictable relations between cause and effect, to rely on and orient ourselves. (Snowden & Boone, 2007).

Diversity: There are multiple and diverse stakeholders affected by the burning issue. Inviting them to co-create the change will be necessary for success.

If these conditions are not present, I do not offer Dialogic OD. I often tell my clients: if "a person with a calculator" can provide a good enough answer for the problem, do not engage people in being part of an unnecessary conversation or process. People like to make real contributions and do not like wasting their time or feeling manipulated. Participatory and dialogic methods should be applied only when the complexity or disruption makes them the shortest and most effective process, or sometimes the only process, that can succeed. If you use dialogic process when it is not necessary you create fatigue and a drop in energy, and if you use it as manipulation—it backfires.

If lengthy periods of complexity and disruption are 'the new normal,' two major questions need to be addressed:

- How do we create conditions to explore complex reality in a comprehensive enough and yet rapid enough mode?
- How do we create the human relationships and the trust needed for meaning-making and wise action during disruptions?

In short, a Dialogic OD process addresses complex situations creatively because of the exploratory nature of a dialogic mindset. We invite the wisdom of the whole system and generate change through emergent structures and processes, enabling them to meet complexity with its intellectual, emotional, and social challenges where intense collective alignment, meaning-making and action are needed.

In generative change processes people are invited to self-organize to pursue a shared purpose (Bushe, 2020). Starting from the first call made by a prospective client, all the way to hosting a dialogic generative process, we engage with the client system as we enter and cross a series of thresholds. This book describes what awaits us beyond each threshold and offers a model of the emergent work-process consultants go through with their clients. The Swirling Spiral Model, presented in the following chapter, is my theory of practice for entering, contracting and engaging with the client organization in a dialogic and emergent process.

TWO

Swirling Spiral Model of Emergent Change

An emergent dialogic process is quite structured, yet since it is different from what we are used to (it's more fluid and interactional), many people will not recognize the structure. In Dialogic OD, some of the structure is planned yet the interactions themselves create a self-organized swirl, a strong and widening energetic field of interactions and relations around a developing shared purpose. This looks quite different from planned change with concrete, predetermined targets that are assigned top-down to people and teams.

This chapter presents a model that captures how I think as I enter an organization and work with people in an emergent dialogic process. This model provides the conceptual scaffolding for understanding the practical issues I cover in later chapters. What is written in this chapter **is not** the language I speak with my clients. It is the language I use to make my work understood to someone who is not present in the situation, the language I teach with. Life experience is always richer and more nuanced than any model. I hope the stories in chapters 4-7 will acquaint you with the actual practice, the living model, with its many faces.

The Swirling Spiral Model describes individual and collective energy evoked through the entry process, making both the personally unique and unifying life energies available for work. Working through the Swirling Spiral creates an energetic structure and flow that supports the consultant and organizational members in developing the relationships and shared understandings and infrastructures needed to work dialogically.

Figure 1:The Swirling Spiral Model of Initiating Emergent Change

The model is a spiral shape, swirling up in widening concentric circles around an attracting center. The graphic image in Figure 1 portrays an energetic, rather than solid, structure that holds the process together. Though subtle and in constant motion, this structure supports co-creation by different people around a shared purpose, evoking intense creative energy to build a future together. The released abundance of life energy self-organizes to meet challenges of holding complexity and the anxiety of not knowing for as long as needed while embracing the unpredictable nature of coping with an adaptive challenge.

One reason I like this image is that it helps us remember the true nature of structure in Dialogic OD. Unlike solid containers that hold what is in them by drawing a boundary between 'in' and 'out'—a boundary that is drawn and held by authority—this 'dancing figure' is an energetic field in constant motion. Here the field is formed by the attraction of the force in the center (axis)—the *shared purpose.* It is held together by the choice-full and authentic participation of an ever-widening group of people and supported by loosely held temporary structures I call *circles of engagement.*

Working through the Swirling Spiral Model

Three main components construct the model:

1. **The Central Axis of shared purpose.** To use the language of complexity, this represents the strange attractor pulling people into the change process. It explains *why* they are willing to invest time and effort. The central axis is the most stable component of the model around which emergent outcomes are created. Yet, its specific content evolves and changes as the change process develops and expands.
2. **The Spiral Form of entry into widening circles.** At each phase of entry, an ever-widening group of people become engaged in the OD process. Figure 2, p. 24, depicts the common sequence of widening circles. It starts with the Caller, proceeds to the Sponsor, the management team, and a diverse planning team, eventually engaging the whole system. Each circle of engagement marks the successful completion of a developmental task before moving to the next. Each circle in this sequence includes and transcends the previous one, accelerating the invitation and strengthening the change-making energy field.
3. **The Swirl of co-creative Flow, from presence to emergent outcomes.** The Swirl attempts to capture the core elements that generate the life energy and self-organizing processes enabling people to creatively meet the burning issue (an adaptive challenge people care about). The Swirl describes the flow of co-creation within each circle. As in Figure 3 below, a swirl is a flow from authentic presence to the emergent outcomes in each circle. The swirl pattern repeats itself in every circle, though the outcomes are unique to each circle.

The Central Axis of shared purpose—Why do it?

The central axis is what powers, attracts, brings people together, and integrates the collective effort. The central axis often appears first as a burning issue and is developed into a shared intention/purpose.

The Shared purpose contributes two forces to the generative process (Bushe, 2020):

1. **Convergent force**: when people choose to join and are attracted to a shared purpose, they are more likely to self-organize in ways that meet and support the common good. The shared purpose usually serves both as a strange attractor for people and as a north star, providing a sense of belonging and directionality. It integrates rich, diverse ideas to meet the purpose.

2. **Divergent force**: by being phrased as a currently desired state of doing, the shared purpose leaves room for joining in experimentation and for self-initiated action. It also leaves room for emergence and further development of the purpose statement itself, as the process unfolds.

According to Bushe (2020), purpose describes what we are trying to do every day to meet an adaptive challenge. A purpose does not delineate a specific measurable achievement in a specific time in the future (this he calls vision/goal) but rather points a clear direction in how we want things to be.

A purpose must be embraced by the sponsor, integrating the organizational challenge and need with the needs and aspirations of the people who will be a part of the change. When this is done artfully the purpose becomes a shared purpose, connecting to the higher and wider good: the wellness of one and all in the wider ecosystem.

The SPIRAL form of Entry in widening circles—Who are the right people and how do we engage them?

The exact number of circles differs depending on circumstances. Figure 2 portrays the expanding circles, starting at the bottom and working up. Entry and contracting happen over and over again at each circle of engagement. While the monetary contract will have been completed by the time we get to the planning team, the psychological contract is still in the making. In the following description of the initial circles of engagement, I identify their developmental task (which is underlined) and the person/people involved (which is capitalized):

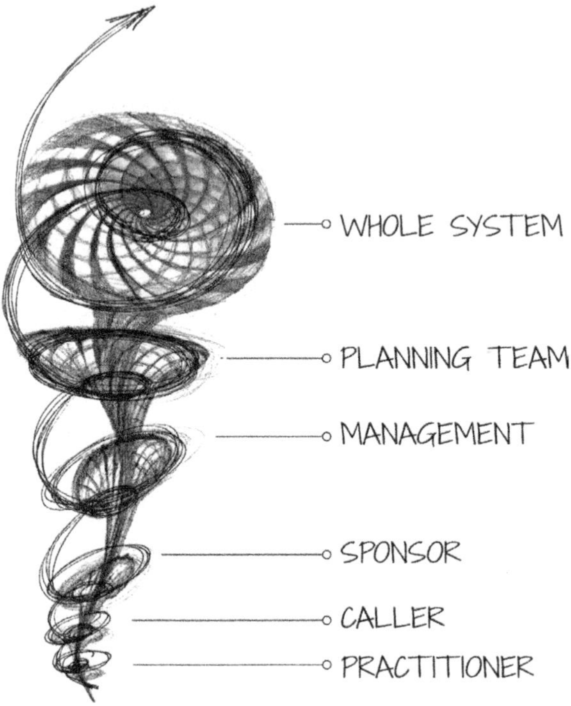

Figure 2: The Spiral Form—widening circles of engagement

Embodying a dialogic stance by the PRACTITIONER

This circle is your growth and development circle as a dialogic person and professional. As dialogic practitioners, we need a high level of social, emotional, and spiritual intelligence. We need the capacity to stay intellectually open, curious, trusting, and in beginner's mind when facing complexity. We need to be authentic and dare to be vulnerable, speaking truth to power when needed. We need to manage our own anxiety and serve as a grounding anchor to the anxiety of others when it is activated. We need to embody the ethics of caring and compassion, holding the intention to be of service for a better future for one and all. Therefore, the Dialogic OD professional engages in a lifelong journey of self-knowing and understanding, increasing capacity for deep listening, empathy, and compassion with self and others while respecting each one and the whole.

Aligning with the CALLER

Sometimes the caller is simply someone who has been asked to gather a list of service providers, a gatekeeper that we must get past to get to the next circle. Most of the time, the caller is the first person to see a need in the organization and connect it to an opportunity. That kind of caller often embodies the passion and senses the potential for Dialogic OD to serve the needs of the organization. The first type of Caller serves as a bridge connecting the consultant with the organization for professional assistance. The latter usually becomes a central ally we partner with throughout the project's duration.

Developing a Covenant Relationship with the SPONSOR

The sponsor is the person in charge, with formal power over the issue at hand. The one accountable for a burning issue without a good enough answer. The sponsor has a key role in the change process and is our primary ally. S/he is the one who chooses whether to follow a prescribed and top-down process or an emergent and participatory one, setting the stage with their intention, invitation, and presence. Developing a covenant relationship with the sponsor in an uncertain and complex context is critical as support and anchor because in these situations, anxiety is high and the terms of engagement cannot be fully known and specified in advance. Covenant goes beyond simple alliance or partnership. Covenant relationship means we commit to be there to support the shared purpose, each other, and the whole system and ecosystem in pursuit of a better future for one and all.

Engaging with the MANAGEMENT TEAM.

The management team who report to the sponsor are usually in charge of the day-to-day line of command in their respective areas/units of operation. We want to meet and engage them in understanding and supporting a generative change process. We want their support in creating a planning team and in co-owning the process with this diverse multi-stakeholder team.

Co-owning with a multi-stakeholder PLANNING TEAM

The planning team, also called the steering committee, design team, or other names, is a group of diverse stakeholders who design, invite, lead and host the dialogic process for the whole system. It does this best when it reflects the diversity of the whole system and is given considerable power and freedom to act.

Depending on the size and the scope of the project and the system, the circles (caller, sponsor, management, planning team) may overlap. This can happen when the scope of work is small, the situation is urgent, or when a continuous trusted relationship between the client system and consultant exists.

The following circles are not the focus of this book, though entering and contracting are involved in every beginning. They are described here just to give a full picture of the spiraling dialogic process.

Co-Creating with the WHOLE SYSTEM

The 'whole system' consists of the people and institutions connected to the issue at hand who have a stake in the change process. You can think of this as the ecosystem of all those relevant, formally and informally, affecting and affected by it (Weisbord and Janoff, 2000).

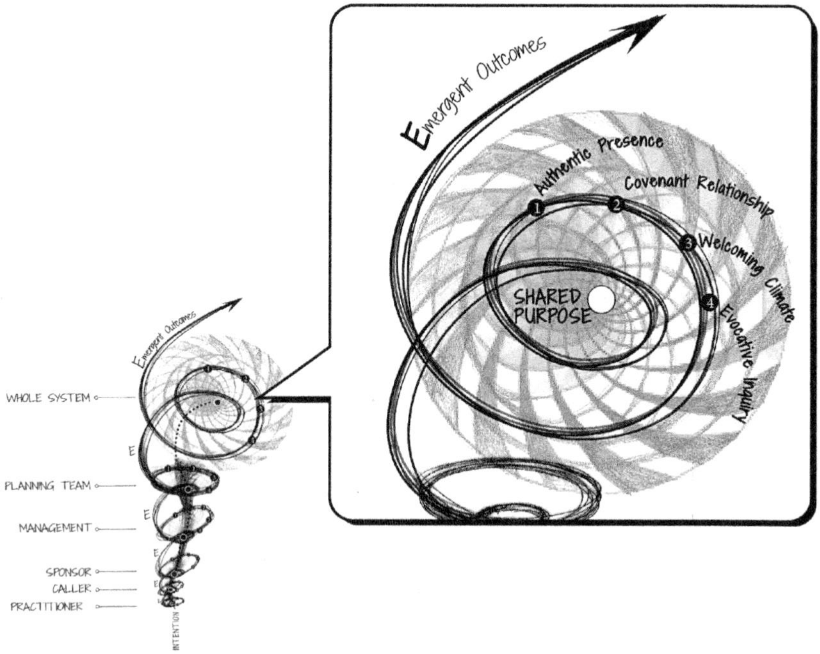

Figure 3: The Swirl pattern of creative flow

Amplifying in the SYSTEM AND THE ECOSYSTEM

This is the process of paying attention to the effect of dialogic events on the wider organization, community, and surrounding ecosystem, and deliberately nurturing, amplifying, and scaling up the results of generative conversations.

Embedding the change and Embodying the DIALOGIC CULTURE

Embedding the outcomes of emergent change means screening the organizational routines and infrastructures for consistency with the emergent changes of the process. If the client system chooses so, they also work to embody the dialogic way of being and doing in day-to-day organizational life by creating a learning community, practicing to co-evolve, and become more adaptive and agile than before.

The SWIRL Motion of creative flow—How to generate life energy for co-creation

The Swirl is a fractal pattern of movement, illustrated in Figure 3, p. 26, which repeats itself in each engagement circle of the spiral. Simply described, the Swirl is the creative motion from presence to emergent outcomes in each circle. It starts from an attractive shared purpose. Many variables influence the movement from presence to outcomes in the context of a shared purpose. The model in Figure 3 identifies the four that I find always show up in my work: Authentic dialogic presence (I), covenant relationships (you), welcoming climate (we), and evocative inquiry (field). I will describe each of these in detail below. My conclusion from years of practice is that being fully and intentionally present in a dialogic stance and beginner's mind serve as a generator of all the other components. Authentic dialogic presence in beginner's mind has the most potential to generate desired collective outcomes if used intentionally by the practitioner, the caller, and the sponsor with the awareness of the swirl pattern of creative flow.

The core of the swirl motion begins when each individual in that circle makes an informed choice to join others in pursuing a shared purpose. I describe what happens next as a set of steps—this is an oversimplification. Some of it will happen in parallel and sometimes we will have to backtrack to develop a deeper relationship, climate, or inquiry. Yet, in general, there is a pattern to the process of doing the work in each circle of entry that the Swirl attempts to capture—a process that begins with how you show up and completes when outcomes emerge that move the system toward accomplishing its purpose of generating a better future on wider aspects.

Embodying One's Authentic Dialogic Presence—the Engine of the Swirl

An authentic dialogic presence has several important attributes.

One is the dialogic mindset that Bushe & Marshak (2015, free Companion to the BMI Series in Dialogic OD) have been elaborating and refining. They describe the dialogic mindset as a set of assumptions about the nature of organizations, leadership, and change. Another aspect of authentic dialogic presence are the dialogic relational skills of acceptance and empathy (Schein, 1988, 2009).

Here I will focus on a different aspect, on our authentic, fully human, and vulnerable presence in beginner's mind.

Why is your signature authentic presence important?

It is through our **authentic presence** that we, as leaders and consultants,

- Create strong, trustworthy relationships.
- Infuse a spirit of colaborative and co-creative inquiry.
- Demonstrate that good ideas can emerge from anywhere.
- Create courageous spaces for people to venture into the unknown.

What does an authentic dialogic presence look like?

We embody an authentic presence by being intentionally truthful at all times, choosing courage over comfort, and daring to be vulnerable. That includes staying open and welcoming to everything and everyone we meet, embracing disruptions, offering humbly what we know, curious about what we do not know, and reframing problems into possibilities on the way to desired futures.

Being in authentic presence is a way of life

Showing up in authentic presence means committing to be true to yourself, to others, and to the way you see things emerge. Daring to be authentic may evoke the fear of not being liked, of guilt, of being shamed—thrown out of belonging (Averbuch, 2011). What if they do not like the way I am? What if what I say is intimidating, offensive, or hurtful to someone? That is less likely to happen if we position our authenticity in a dialogic stance—an authentic intention to be helpful, using our whole true self in service of the situation.

Choosing to be authentic may make us feel exposed and evoke feelings of vulnerability, the emotion that we feel in face of uncertainty, risk, and emotional exposure (Brown, 2012). According to Brown, vulnerability is measured by the courage to show up as you are when you do not know the consequence and cannot control the outcome. I find that to be an accurate description of the context of dialogic work. Brown suggests, and I deeply agree, feeling vulnerable is not a weakness. In fact, it demonstrates the courage to risk showing up in the arena, engaging as yourself in situations with consequences you cannot predict, ready to embrace embarrassment and failure as part of your way, and welcome feedback from other players in the arena.

So why should you show up in your authenticity and vulnerability?

- **Choosing authenticity helps you share the client's vulnerability.** During generative change the sponsor and the client system are in vulnerable situations because they have to act when unable to control the outcomes. Your willingness to be vulnerable not only acts as a role model but also creates a sense of 'being in this together'.
- **Choosing authenticity makes you more likely to be respected and trusted.** By showing up authentically, you demonstrate that you will not put 'fitting-in' or the paycheck ahead of your beliefs. People will trust and respect you because they can count on you to tell them the truth and do what is right. Authenticity and vulnerability create genuine contact (Williams, 2007) and a possibility for rapidly creating intimacy and trust even with highly cynical and suspicious people.

- **Choosing authenticity allows for imperfection and playful experimentation.** People are relieved when they are accepted for who they really are. They can let go of the habit of 'being right' and being righteous. This results in a welcoming and nourishing climate of playful and joyful experimentation—without blame, or judgment (Arrien, 1993)—creating a resilient culture that is equipped to deal with whatever comes its way. Allowing for diversity in style, perceptions, and opinions, accepting mistakes as valuable information, and enabling the creative flow of innovation. No vulnerability equals no creativity. Similarly, no tolerance for failure leads to no innovation.
- **Choosing authenticity brings out the signature value that only you can offer.** Authenticity brings out uniqueness: There is no one in the world that can be better than you in being you. Who you are, what you know, how you make sense of what is taking place around you—these are the things where you add value as only you can.
- **Choosing authenticity helps you to know yourself and evolve.** To be authentic is to be aware of your moment-to-moment experience, aware of what you are sensing, observing, thinking, feeling, and wanting (Bushe, 2009). Noticing what we are experiencing and doing and working to align those to our values and ethics creates a continuous cycle of improvement. It helps in becoming who you aspire to be. This is an infinite journey in which you are constantly evolving. As you come to terms with yourself, it is contagious, and people around you become more at ease with themselves, making all of us better.
- **Choosing authenticity is choosing to see and be seen.** When we allow ourselves to really be seen we get a real sense of belonging (the way we genuinely are) without compromising ourselves, by trying to 'fit in' (Brown, 2012). This is a true path to vitality, love, and joy in our professional as well as our personal lives.

From a very young age, I experienced myself as a person who does not really have the choice of whether to be authentic to myself and others (Averbuch, 2011). My learning-living edge was to figure out how I could be authentic without destroying relationships or scaring people away. Here is a story of what I learned about **giving authentic feedback**:

> As a newly-minted OD consultant I used to begin every intervention in the following way: interview all relevant people, form a diagnosis, and feed it back to the client. Oddly enough, I noticed that some of the clients were deeply hurt by what I thought to be positive and empowering feedback. Others, getting challenging feedback, were very happy and thankful. My colleagues and I interpreted this by labeling the first group 'defensive' while the latter were labeled 'open'. I was looking for a better explanation, preferably one that I could influence.
>
> Five years later I found a key!: the more I was speaking from a loving place in myself, truly connected—in the moment—to the part in me that wanted the best for them, I could say any feedback and it would be accepted as a generous gift. The more I was not present in my love and care for them while giving the feedback, even complements were at risk of sounding like a judgment and ill-received.

I was surprised and happy to crack this riddle, so I brought it home as well.

Beginner's mind

Another aspect of primary authenticity to develop and embody, is the childlike beginner's mind. We need beginner's mind (Suzuki, 1995) all along the dialogic process because of the disruptive nature of its context and emergent nature of its process.

Showing up in beginner's mind means staying curious and fresh, highly impressionable, and full of awe and wonder like a newborn or an adult in a very foreign country. Humble with what we know and offer, alert and receptive to ecosystem, listening, inquiring, assuming very little (Schein, 2009). Entering a beginner's state of mind requires an open and receiving attitude. We put aside (at least momentarily for the interaction) what we know, think, and feel. Gendlin describes this in the process of *Focusing*: tuning in to listen to your *felt sense,* creating room to pay attention, and listen, and invite life energy to move forward by doing so (Gendlin, 2007). With beginner's mind we are ready to open to deep listening beyond our own pre-conceptions and historical ways of making sense. When we hold our opinions, assumptions, and ideas lightly, we are ready to listen to nuances and embrace what seems to have more life and potential than our own idea, drawn to what has wisdom, life, and beauty. And when we are ready to entertain what seems impossible at first sight, we will experience and exercise the sense of freedom, joy, and creativity of beginner's mind. Luckily beginner's mind is contagious by nature. Hopefully, others will step into this presence and mindset with us, creating a possibility for an evocative, self-organized field of inquiry for the challenge we face.

To illustrate, let me tell you a story about authentic presence and beginner's mind.

> It is seven o'clock in the morning on the second day of an engaged and fruitful 420 person open space gathering. We are arranging the room and I find out we are missing four summaries of yesterday's break-out sessions. I can't believe it. Seven years of Large Group Interventions and it had never happened before. After searching in the room and inside myself, I feel shame and helplessness. Reminding myself of the open space dictum "whatever happens is the only thing that could have," I start getting curious. I decide to open the morning news with this. After a few minutes of good mornings and check-in I say: "Our work yesterday was very fruitful. The proceedings are in the booklet on your seat. I am embarrassed to say that a few summaries did not make it to this booklet. I am not sure what happened, this has never happened to me before." Of course, I asked people to see if their summary was missing and invited them to restore or recreate the missing summaries. I continued: "When I realized this morning that a few summaries are missing, I went through feelings of shame, guilt, and failure. Then I asked myself, if I choose to look at life as an ongoing draft and adopt the principle 'whatever happens is the only thing that could have'—I get curious. Assuming all of us were taking responsibility and trying our best—what could be the meaning of making this shameful mistake in this gathering? What can it be telling us? I need your help trying to answer this." I hoped sharing the truth transparently and offering to become curious (beginner's mind) would take us somewhere meaningful, but I was unsure whether anyone would speak, attack, or? I was out on a limb. 420 people were sitting in concentric circles around me, and the room was silent. I held the mic and looked all around to see if anyone wanted to speak. After what seemed like a long silence, people started to talk about their system as being a 'knowing' system, a 'never make a mistake' system, the shame in learning, and so on. This went on for about 15

minutes of speaking truth from the heart and mind. Searching instead of shaming and blaming. What a joy.

Three hours later the missing summaries were found, printed, and shared.

As your presence is established as a clear and embodied dialogic identity in action, creating a sound relational base becomes naturally easy.

Covenant Relationship—Why is it a critical step for walking an unknown path together?

To withstand disruptions, uncertainty, and vulnerability, a special type of relationship is needed. Alliance, Partnership, and Covenant are three different types of human bonding and social contracting that I use to describe the consultant-client relationship. A covenant type of relationship is best suited to Dialogic OD.

When we think of contracting, as in alliance or legal partnership, we mostly think of a transactional relationship where what we will give and get is spelled out and contingent on one another. Alliance and partnership are types of relationships performed as a series of *finite games*. Finite games operate under specific conditions with predetermined rules and consequences, assuming we can foresee future events in which they will take place (Carse, 1986; Sinek 2019).

What I am calling a **'covenant'** is not transactional but rather transformational by nature. It's a relationship where one takes vows for the long haul. In any complex, emergent reality, terms cannot be contingently specified since we don't know what will unfold. Covenant language offers to commit not only to one another (horizontal dimension) but also to 'a shared path', our shared higher intentions (vertical dimension). This is a deep commitment to oneself, to other/s, and to a wider cause. Therefore, covenant relations reflect core values that define who you are and who you aspire to become.

The following story illustrates a common expression of covenant relationships between consultant and sponsor from my work with Ntech.

Listening to the sponsors' expectations and organizational needs as they moved from a startup to a mature organization, I was convinced

> of their sincere intention to help the organization move on. I noted that when we embark on such a process, we never know where it may take us, adding that I would like to start the process with understanding what would happen if they reach the conclusion that the person who needs to lead the organization is not one of them. Both of them said: "That would be fine!" Yet I insisted on creating the time and space to really think what would a meaningful life look like, professionally and personally, if they were no longer in the CEO role in this organization. I said: "We may not need it, but we need to know that you are safe." Working this issue could be seen as outside the scope of the problem (make a million dollars to save the company) I had been hired for. Yet feeling it is my duty and privilege to see them, as people, and to be in covenant with each one of them as well as with the common good, it seemed important that we spent time following this evocative line of inquiry.

Covenant is an *infinite game,* not bound by predetermined rules. There is no designated time and space to crown winners or losers since we cannot foresee future events in complex and edge of chaos situations. Everyone is invited to join the game (Carse, 1986; Sinek 2019). Organization Development, as a discipline, has always aspired to act in the best interests of more than just the person signing the checks. A covenant carries the promise to take care of whatever will emerge in the wider system, mindful of one and all.

When going into the unknown together, people need more than a legal or 'quid pro quo' contract; they need a covenant type of commitment. Logic by itself does not provide answers when a leap of faith is needed. As authentic and vulnerable presence are shared in covenant relationships, a welcoming and enabling climate is created.

Welcoming Climate—What is the gift of a welcoming climate?

A welcoming climate is an atmosphere in which everyone can feel they belong, and are welcomed and accepted as they are. It is the ground for trust and calm in collective conduct. A welcoming climate is built gradually through genuine invitations, full inclusion of people who are passionate to participate, appreciation of diversity, and ensuring that all voices are heard. There are many ways, subtle and not so, that show people they are welcome. Creating a welcoming climate is the art of weaving a fabric of home and community in organizations.

A welcoming climate is created when leaders embody an authentic presence and inspire us all to bring our authentic selves. Cynicism fades away, as does shaming and insult. This gives space for expressing who we are and what we feel, think and want without the need to be on guard all the time. When embracing mistakes, if good humor and playfulness are present, people dare to experiment, falling and rising like infants while learning to walk. It may be frustrating, but it is all in the context of growing and finding the way together.

A welcoming climate serves as a cradle for the emergence of an evocative, and often decentralized, field of inquiry where new learning takes place.

Evocative Inquiry—What is enabled by evocative, decentralized inquiry?

Focused on the shared purpose that brings us together, we want to open a space that allows for sensing into multiple directions, experimenting with various ideas, exploring, curious and learning, increasing generativity and the creation of new ideas people will want to act on. I call this stage 'evocative inquiry'. The Dialogic OD practitioner's responsibility is to help frame questions that draw people into new, surprising, unexplored, and bold directions. When working one-on-one, as in a coaching or personal consultancy situation, this involves helping the caller or sponsor explore new pathways for themselves or new perspectives on the situation. When working with larger systems, this involves stimulating multiple lines of inquiry simultaneously in a decentralized, mostly self-organized, way.

A decentralized field of inquiry is like an octopus, an intelligent creature with a distributed brain whose different arms explore its surroundings independently. Unlike a centralized field that needs things to be planned, sequenced and fit together in logical congruence, a decentralized field promotes multiple and simultaneous inquiries, numerous experiments initiated by whoever cares to act on a shared issue. It's the shared issue and purpose that provides the connective tissue among all the activities, and the welcoming climate and covenant relationships that provide the connective tissue among people. A decentralized field of engaged and interconnected people can embrace disruption, lean into uncertainty, tolerate conflicting data and paradoxes while postponing judgment and avoiding overly simple solutions because a shared purpose, leaders living a dialogic presence, and authentic covenant relationships can hold the field together until clarity emerges.

Emergent Outcomes of New Meaning, Actions and People's Web of Connections (MAP)

Emergent outcomes are the offspring of self-organization by engaged people in interaction. The outcomes are not predictable in content or time and space, yet if we follow this Swirl from authentic presence to evocative Inquiry, outcomes that move the organization closer to its shared purpose are bound to emerge. And, more often than not, they will be accompanied by other emergent/surprising outcomes that will support the organization's transformation. Outcomes such as new narratives, new shared meanings, a wide range of new possibilities, a sense of alignment and belonging coupled by a feeling of being alive spreads among people. New threads of acquaintances, partnerships and friendships are seeded and created. **I refer to this as a new MAP:**

- Shared **M**eaning
- Aligned **A**ctions
- Web of **P**eople, partnerships, and friendships

All three dimensions of the MAP strengthen the human fabric of belonging and organizing, feeding resilience and the ability to creatively meet any problem or disruptions yet to come.

THREE

Beginnings and Endings

Every beginning is a unique and powerful moment that often encapsulates the essence of what's to come. Like a sprouting seed, it carries both the intensity of life pushing to be materialized and the blueprint of the potential nature of this specific life. Beginning, like any infancy, is an amplifying and fragile time. Since the order that emerges out of chaos is strongly influenced by initial conditions, we have to be mindful of first impressions and the imprints they embed. Though generative change transforms much faster than top-down processes, the fluid nature of emergence and generative conversations demand careful attention in the early stages to assure they survive the inevitable push from participants, and pull from leaders, toward the known, controlled, and expected. Since generative change requires an inquiring and innovating rather than problem-solving stance, you need to show up with an embodied and nuanced dialogic presence if you want to have transformative interactions with the client system. If you are seen and initially labeled as 'a usual consultant', it will be harder to propose a new way of being and doing change in the organization. Foster authenticity, vulnerability, diversity, and ambiguity from the beginning.

This chapter explores some differences between dialogic and diagnostic approaches to beginnings, describing the unique nature of generative change as a never-ending beginning. Entering each circle in the spiral of widening engagement is a new beginning for us and everyone in the circle. Doing the swirl work around purpose, from presence to outcomes, in each Swirl requires a beginner's fresh and curious mind and a heart full of potential.

Beginnings

Take a moment to lean back and invite your own wisdom, what you already know about entering an organization/beginning a project. I invite you to stay a while with the following questions:

- What does beginning mean to you, what picture or metaphor do you hold for initial connection with the organization?
- What is your usual pattern of beginning a process as an external/internal OD practitioner?
- What are you noticing about yourself? About your beginnings in general and in generative change processes in particular?

The Beginning Process in Diagnostic versus Dialogic OD Mindsets

The term 'beginning' is most often defined as the point in time and space at which something starts. I use the word 'beginning' in two ways: As initial stages of something—what comes first; and as a state of mind—full of possibilities, fresh and curious—a beginner's mind.

As consultants, we usually begin an intervention to assist in addressing an undesired reality or to prepare for future demands. When we are invited—or offer—to help a system, we are usually asked to submit a proposal that describes what we are offering after a short orientation by the client. When the potential client states the problem, looking for a process to create the answer, they may have in mind various types of dialogic, or most of the time, diagnostic consultants.

Beginning in a **diagnostic mindset** is usually a straightforward process in terms of people and time. By the end of it, you know your goals, you know what you want to achieve, and you have stated the expected results. You start systematically, usually a top-down, linear process—management first and the rest will follow. The beginning is short, yet implementation may take forever.

Beginning in a **dialogic mindset** is, in my experience, a more winding process, larger in scope of people and time. By the end of it, there are principles and a rough draft of stages in the process and relationships that you can trust to withstand and support going together into the unknown—the unfolding and emerging future process. There is clarity of purpose and intention yet no clear picture of the actual specific process that will be used or the results that will follow. The beginning process is a bit longer, yet implementation is interwoven into the participatory process where people create the understanding, the conversation, and the leadership to act in an aligned and immediate way.

Remember—our initial way of being and doing as Dialogic OD consultants serves both as a well-needed disruption to the old way of entering and contracting and as a collective 'tuning fork' of the whole process. If we enter and contract dialogically—with clear intention, not knowing in advance exactly where we are heading, equal and co-creative—our unique presence will come as a surprise to the client. This surprise is useful since it usually creates a pause needed for reorienting the client. "Hey, what is going on here? This is not what I am used to...what do you mean when you say you don't know?" We start from a fresh and adventurous place. Yes, we will be challenged as practitioners in a performance-oriented world yet experienced as a fresh alternative to the traditional 'change making' process. It has happened many times in my practice. People remember their surprise at my authentically saying what I know and what I don't. They recall I was not trying to sell or persuade or prove I was best or better. Rather, I approached as an ally and co-creator to figure out what is needed and what will best serve.

A variety of scientific and intuitive sources teach us about the critical nature of beginnings:

Chaos theory teaches us that initial conditions can shape what emerges out of chaos:

Dialogic OD processes are mostly needed in complex situations when the emergence of new order is required. Lorenz, a mathematician experimenting with weather forecasting, coined the term 'butterfly effect', meaning that a small change in initial conditions leads to a much greater difference later on (Holman, 2015). Lorenz teaches us that when order grows out of chaos, it is greatly influenced by threshold/initial conditions.

Cultural expressions and ceremonial acts teach us that beginnings tell a lot about what follows:

Common wisdom teaches us to start "with the right foot"; the initial energy as we wake up in the morning may "paint" our day for better or worse. We have shared cultural meanings and manners of beginning, and we create expectations in ourselves and others by how we begin. Ceremonies and rituals are used in all societies to cross thresholds of beginnings—such as the life passages of birth, marriage, and death—in an attempt to equip them with what is necessary for the specific passage and to bless them with good fortune. (Driver, 1991)

Developmental psychological research teaches us that beginnings are critical:

Pregnancy and the first months and years of life are considered formative. They influence biological and psychological development, setting directions for whom an individual becomes (Rutter, 2002). Initial environmental conditions, such as space, light, loving welcome, sense of belonging, influence what emerges in a baby's life, a classroom, a home, or a large group gathering. First impressions are proven to be most influential on future relationships in all of life (Human et al., 2013).

Why are Beginnings, as a state of 'Beginner's Mind', important?

My preferred way to look at the emergent Dialogic OD change process is as an ongoing beginning. In a beginning, our minds are open, fresh, curious, and ready.

In 'Zen Mind, Beginner's Mind' Shunaryu Suzuki beautifully says: "In the beginner's mind there are many possibilities, but in the expert's mind there are few" (1995, p 21). Beginner's mind is limitless, empty, open and ready. Suzuki adds: "when we have no thoughts of achievement, no thoughts of self, we are true beginners. The beginner's mind is the mind of compassion….it is the secret of the arts: always be a beginner" (1995, p 21). This perfectly describes the beginner's mind I believe is needed for the art and craft of Dialogic OD.

Beginner's mind is important in Dialogic OD because any beginning, initial stage, is a complex and unpredictable situation. When you enter an organization, you are trying to orient yourself, figuring out the place, the people, and the issue. Trying to sort out what to ask and what to tell about yourself and your work that will be appropriate and useful. Both you and the client are in a sensing and testing mode. You need to read the situation rapidly and adjust to different people's needs and style while, in most cases, presenting a dialogic paradigm they are not familiar with. For instance:

> In our first meeting ever, it was odd to tell the Major General, who was looking for a better way to create a long-term strategic plan, that "No, I am not a strategy expert nor an army expert, but I can help you design and facilitate processes that bring together the whole system to discuss and co-create your strategic direction for the coming 20 years in an about 6 month process ....That is my expertise". As I was talking, I was aware that I could be thrown out of the office or win the project, which I did.

Beginner's mind is important in Dialogic OD because any emergent process is a never-ending beginning. Every emergent process has changes, disruptions and surprises. The art is finding a thread to act upon when you are unsure of what is going on and what the right thing to do is. These situations are "a beginning all the way through". Here's an example from the same case:

> On the second and last day of a whole system gathering, we were trying to help the group gain focus. We asked people to choose (with sticky dots) the two most important topics out of thirteen. 150 people reacted in real distress: "We cannot, at least not right now. All of it is important". Being resisted by the group was surprising since the gathering was going so well! Seeing something was stuck, we (the consulting team) paused, created a fishbowl with the Major General and external and internal consultants in the center of the circle of 150 people. A new way to bring focus emerged: "We know all of you are very busy people. Choose two topics that you insist you be actively engaged in." That was easy. Immediately they dived into the task. This reframing removed the obstacle of thinking *about* importance by guiding people to actively *experiencing* what is important. So we flowed again.

Beginner's mind is important in Dialogic OD because navigating complexity requires being fresh, awake, and ready to surprise our-

selves and others. A beginner's attitude keeps us curious and humble, in wonder and immersed, deeply listening and sensing as we interact with 'what is'. We lean into our inquiring, exploring, courageous and experimental edge rather than our knowing, comfortable zone. Beginner's mind and attitude are critical for surviving and navigating complexity where there is no apparent pattern or causality to anchor ourselves. Here is another story from the same process:

> When he returned from taking care of a sad emergency, how could I create a new beginning with the Major General and create a smooth continuation with the 150 people who had already been working? Because he didn't attend the first part of the opening circle, and was not familiar with dialogue principles where people in plenary only talk to the center and don't respond to each other, the Major General was using a traditional conversational pattern of gracefully responding to everyone who spoke in the large circle, inadvertently disempowering everyone else. Beginner's mind was the answer! Before I knew it, I danced into the middle of the circle and, in a childlike manner, said, "I feel the space is a little closed. Let me open it a bit more." I spread my arms in an airplane shape and 'flew' drawing with my steps the circle line, vocalizing the sound of an airplane engine and saying: "I am re-opening the space for everyone to talk to the center." Sound crazy? In a way it was. Yet, it created a mode of conversation in which everyone, including the Major General, were now talking to the center (and the permission to act 'crazy' in service of our shared purpose).

Beginner's mind is important in Dialogic OD because beginnings are natural settings to learn how to work with uncertainty and disruption and practice a dialogic mindset and principles. We can approach beginnings from a well-planned, goal-oriented, knowing-what-is-right mindset or come not knowing, curious, and ready to be changed by the situation, bringing our experiences, expertise, and skills to design and hold a process of finding out. We can show up with humility, engagement, and curiosity to co-create (Schein, 2009).

Since beginnings are an inescapable time and place to meet the unknown, they can consciously serve as the natural space for experiencing and managing the emotions that arise in disrupted and uncertain situations. They help train us to embody dialogic principles in emergent processes. One last bit of the story:

> During the initial stages of this army process, there were several times I was ready to leave. Here is one: I believe the sponsor has to make the invitation to dialogic events, yet they said that an invitation signed by the Major General is 'an order'. I was ready to quit right there, explaining that for self-organization to occur, we need agency; people need to have a real choice. As I shared my thoughts and feelings of stuckness, a deeper search started in the planning team. They came up with a colorful 'crazy' invitation signed by the Major General yet making clear, both in shape and content, indicating this was a very different invitation and engagement.

The most important thing to understand about beginnings is that they are highly impressionable and formative, like the first years of life. If you do it well, it has the highest return on investment you will ever have.

This book focuses on getting started, yet some say that "you have to begin with the end in mind". That is certainly true of managers asking for assistance. We are often asked, "OK, I get it, but how can I be sure that after all the gathering and fun we will have concrete necessary results?" In other words, what does the ending and outcomes of a dialogic process look like? How is it different from the Diagnostic OD process?

Endings and outcomes

Dialogic and diagnostic mindsets offer a very different perception on endings and outcomes.

With a **diagnostic mindset,** the ending is usually perceived as termination. Results are usually predetermined. When embarking on a consulting **project**, we are asked to state the actual outputs or results we will deliver and how they will be measured against predetermined goals and objectives.

With a **dialogic mindset,** the ending is perceived as a continuation or transformation from working with a consultant to working independently. As to results and outcomes—they are emergent. Emergence is, by definition, the birth place of novelty because predefined outcomes rely only on what is currently understood. As a result, they sub-optimize or preclude the potential of engaging a system in imagining and creating their desired future. When embarking on a consulting **process**, we make it clear that we expect valuable outcomes concerning the problem but they are not, and cannot be, predetermined. Because we are working with emergent processes and content, typically with diverse people from the whole system, more innovative results will occur. We expect change to happen more quickly, but we don't know what exactly it will be. Dialogic process makes more and better possible, though we do not know how the relevant results will unfold or what other surprising outcomes will come into being.

This is the time to ask some seemingly paradoxical questions:

- What are the common/expected outcomes of an emergent dialogic process?

and

- What is unique to outcomes of emergent dialogic processes?

The following story illustrates the different types of emergent outcomes that are common to a generative change process.

INN, a communication-infrastructure company, was in crisis. INN was in its third round of layoffs and was desperate for cash. With a diverse planning team, in less than three months, we designed and held a large group gathering to address the question "How do we make One Million Dollars in this coming year?"

140 people showed up, created an agenda, engaged in deep listening, conversations and meaning-making, and initiated groups formed to detect and address misalignment issues all over the organization.

Even though the CEO opened the gathering announcing there would be another layoff (100 out of the remaining 420), the immediate outcome of the first day was a palpable sense of community.

Let me delineate the outcomes as they were reported to me by Harriet, my colleague that continued to work with the organization (I was brought in only for the large group intervention):

1. During the gathering:

   i. The organization came to life as a community to revive the business.

   ii. A shift from a sense of disaster to a sense of pride to belong to this community of people.

2. Over the next three months:

   i. 320 people who were not laid off did all they could and helped find jobs for 100 friends who did, all of them found new employment.

   ii. Good communication, trust, and cohesiveness helped keep morale high.

3. Over the next six months:

   i. They tried to sell their products with no success. (It was one of my first emergent large group projects. I felt so sorry and guilty at not 'delivering', not understanding why they were so satisfied)

   ii. Better alignment and a sense of belonging and pride gave energy for a difficult struggle resulting in a determination not to give up.

4. Over the next eleven months:

   i. The cohesiveness of this large group of employees enabled the owners to negotiate and successfully sell the firm as "one working enterprise".

   ii. 320 employees were bought by another firm, no one lost their job.

   iii Owners benefited economically.

   iv The acquiring company's stock price rose dramatically (11%)—a major sale of INN communication infrastructures that started eleven months ago materialized that month.

What was considered a goal, a desired outcome, had shifted as well: in this case the adaptive challenge was perceived as sales/money for the organization's survival, but that was temporarily impossible. On the way they discovered that the deeper layer of the adaptive challenge was not the survival of the organization but the survival and wellbeing of all stakeholders. They created a self-organizing strategy that supported that; staying aligned and cohesive in the storm until it was over, probing and committing to any possible venue. With time they discovered a new and higher order: the possibility that an organizational frame can die while all stakeholders thrive, individually and collectively.

Outcomes that we can clearly see here are common results of Dialogic OD processes used when there is a real deeply shared purpose:

Community: Sense of belonging, happy and proud to be part of this community.

Possibility: Increase in energy level. A shift towards vitality, trust, hope, 'can do'.

Covenant relations: Standing for one another, the organization and beyond.

Wise self-organized aligned action: Engagement, commitment and action to detect and do what is in their power to help carry the purpose forward.

Stakeholder's gain: All stakeholders benefit (here: economically and psychologically).

Transformation: New and more complex/coherent organization emerges.

Generative change processes create various emergent outcomes. Some are more visible than others. Often, outcomes are visible in the large

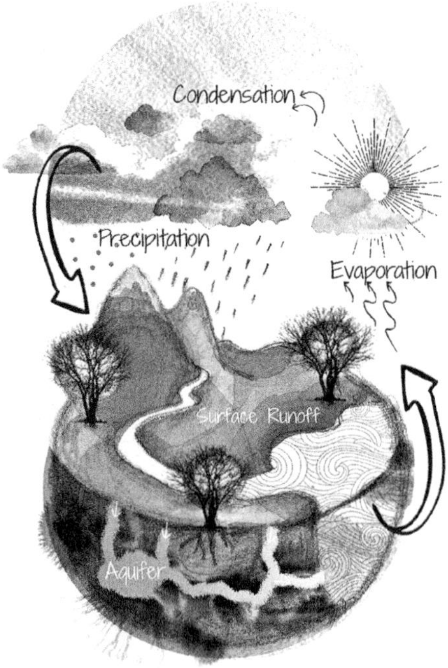

Figure 4: The Water Cycle

group gatherings, then participants lose touch with those they are not directly involved with. Emergent outcomes from throughout the generative change process are like precipitation. Like rain, sometimes it pours and sometimes it drizzles, nourishing little flowers as well as the whole water cycle. Some water stays on the surface, some evaporates and some absorbs into the ground.

Like the water cycle in this metaphor, outcomes can appear on different landscapes:

Outcomes that are seen on the surface. The most visible outcomes typically pertain to the main issue: initiatives, probes, pilot projects, prototypes, and decisions. For example, all of the outcomes listed in the INN story above were seen and acknowledged.

Outcomes that evaporate and may come again. Topics of concern or interest that were brought up by one or a few people and seem impossible or irrelevant may be implemented in a different form or may rise again when the system is ready. For example, some of the employees that were laid off and started working somewhere else gradually made it back to their 'community' in the acquiring organization.

Outcomes that seep deeply into the groundwater and surface as a spring in another time and place. These outcomes are underground streams that feed the aquifer—ideas and connections that people create form personal new experiences and new relationships enabled by dialogic processes. The aquifer absorbs the potential of holding new perceptions of leadership, conversations, co-creation, and future engagement. For example, members of the planning team, who were co-leading this process for half a year or more, ended up in more senior managerial positions as this dialogic and generative process served as their training for management in turbulent times and for ways to face the unknown creatively. For some participants, the whole experience of meeting dialogically will remain a longing they seek to recreate for themselves and others. Sometimes the process changes the course of people's lives and ripples beyond them.

Typically, the surface outcomes are the only ones that most people notice. Oddly, with time, people even seem to forget the origins of these surface outcomes and attribute it to themselves regardless of where it started. To illustrate, here is a story from a year-long process with the ministry of education:

> Nathanial, who participated as a stakeholder in one of a sequence of strategic gatherings of the Ministry of Education, voiced his ideas and was hired to lead a project of recruiting 10,000 needed teachers right away. He called me and said, "I have been interviewing people to get to know the system. All of them do not have enough words to describe how wonderful and groundbreaking the national gathering of 420 people was. Yet they all express disappointment that nothing resulted." My heart dropped. I called my colleague and said, "a beautiful gathering without noticeable concrete results?" As I said this, I realized that his role and operation came into being as a result of this gathering! He—and even I—did not perceive it immediately. It took being 'blamed' with not having concrete results. What a ride.

That conversation taught me a lot about the dissipative nature of **attribution** in emergent processes. When a result is pre-planned, someone holds it long enough to know where it originated, or at least so it is perceived. When an outcome is emergent, one or two things happen. Either it organically blends into the organization without anyone thinking about where it was born. Or, when people are deeply engaged in the work, they attribute the outcomes to themselves, their passion, initiative, and self-organization. They perceive the gathering as an opportunity they were lucky to have experienced. Both perceptions are true and show organic ownership.

Does it matter? Is it important to attribute some of the credit to the gathering as well? I think it is, for both the client system and the practitioner, in few ways:

- Respecting the participants (people who invested time, energy, and personal engagement) who want to know the fruits of their effort by informing the client system what came out of the gathering.
- Building trust in Dialogic OD and generative emergent processes as effective process, with relevant outcomes for the organization and participants.
- Learning the nature of emergent outcomes in participatory self-organizing processes.

- Managing and communicating in a way that keeps the momentum of change alive.

And lastly: it is important for practitioners to know that their presence may be less visible in dialogic emergent methodologies. According to Harrison Owen, creator of Open Space Technology (OST), the effective practitioner is "totally present and absolutely invisible" (Owen, 1997, p.64), does only what is needed and gets out of the way as soon as possible, staying invisibly present for service. McKergow (2020) explores this aspect of 'hosting' Dialogic OD events in great detail.

Be prepared that even in most remembered and appreciated processes, they may not know who you are. An anecdote from my practice illustrates it. Four years after the gathering described above, in an initial conversation exploring a new project, one of its members said: "I know what you are talking about! I have attended something very special that sounds like what you are describing. You would have loved it." He did not recall I facilitated it!

Table 1: Beginnings and Outcomes

Beginnings	
Beginnings are unique and powerful moments, often encapsulating the essence of what's to come. Like a sprouting seed, it carries the intensity of life materializing and a blueprint of the potential for this specific life. *Two definitions of beginning:* *Initial stages—what comes first* *A state of mind—full of possibilities, fresh and curious—a beginner's mind*	• What does beginning mean to me, what picture or metaphor do I hold for initial connection with the organization? • What is my usual pattern of beginning a process as an external/internal OD practitioner? • What am I noticing about myself? About my habitual beginnings in general and in generative change processes in particular?
Beginning in dialogic versus diagnostic mindset	• What does the beginning of a dialogic process look like? • How is it different from the Diagnostic OD process?

Table 1: Beginnings and Outcomes *(continued)*

Outcomes	
Emergent outcomes are like rain. Sometimes it pours and sometimes it drizzles, nourishing flowers as well as the whole water cycle. *Some water stays on the surface, some evaporates, and some absorbs into the ground*	• What are the common/expected outcomes of an emergent dialogic process? (Community, possibility, covenant relationship, self-organized aligned action) • What is unique to outcomes of emergent dialogic processes? • Why is it important to attribute some of the credit to the dialogic process/event as well?

As a concluding note, outcomes in a dialogic process are multi-layered, nourishing the present and the future. Bearing in mind the dissipative nature of emergent outcomes makes leadership AFTER large group gatherings very important (Bushe 2020). Infrastructure and some plans must be in place, before these events, for how emergent outcomes will be noticed, resourced, and communicated to the rest of the system.

And a personal recommendation: if you successfully lead a Dialogic OD process, the people will say, "we did it". Prepare yourself and your road companions for it to be so. Find ways to satisfy the need to be seen and recognized for accomplishments (I started teaching as I felt too invisible as a dialogic consultant☺). Create a structure for closure with the sponsors and the planning team to debrief the experience, share lessons learned, express appreciation, and, perhaps, explore what's next for them now.

PART TWO

Practice: Step by Step

"The things we have to learn before we do them, we learn by doing them..."

—*Aristotle,* The Nicomachean Ethics

FOUR

Readiness: Initial Screening for Suitability

In this chapter we explore three questions on the threshold of entering; all three are explored and decided with the client:

- Is the situation ready?
- Is the client system ready?
- Is the consultant ready?

When I use the term readiness, I mean having, or being able to create, in a relevant time frame, the necessary preconditions to embark on a process. Before we engage in a Dialogic OD process with a new or existing client, or get our first phone call asking us to assist, it is helpful to have some understanding of what **readiness** means in this context. It is also useful to have a notion of how readiness is assessed with the client.

Readiness assessment is an ongoing process that starts the minute the consultant and client meet. Readiness evolves and deepens throughout the Dialogic OD process. This chapter focuses mainly on the readiness we interactively screen for and build in our first few meetings with the client, usually our initial engagement with caller and sponsor circles (fully described in chapter 5).

Initial assessment of readiness for Dialogic OD—Screening for a triple "yes" of Readiness

To check out the possibility of working together, I have an initial conversation with the person who contacts me—the caller—at the pre-entry point. If we mutually decide to proceed, I also have a conversation with the person in charge of the relevant unit/organization—the sponsor. The initial assessment of readiness is intended to let both the client and me know if we can consider working together in general and consider dialogic work in particular. This often starts from pure listening (Schein, 2009). Later on in the conversation I use the following three clusters of questions as a checklist, usually in this sequence:

Present:

- Why are you looking for assistance? Why now?
- What is it that is bothering you? What keeps you sleepless at night?
- What brought you to me?

Past:

- What did you already try and how did it work/didn't work for you?
- What are your past experiences in working with consultants?

Future:

- If I had a magic wand and I could promise you an answer to one question only, a critical and essential question that, if answered, will clear the picture for you and the rest will easily follow... what would this question be?
- Imagine it worked very well, we are after the intervention process and you are happy and satisfied with everything—tell me what is making you so happy? What brought us to this point? What has changed?

As the client and I listen and discuss the answers, we screen the three essential 'C's, : **context—client—consultant**

1. Context—Is the situation ready/suitable?

- Is this an adaptive challenge/wicked problem?
- Is there a *real burning issue* to which no one has a good enough answer?
- Is this a situation that calls for a new and unknown path for which there is no straightforward remedy that is available?

This type of screening provides an impression about both the urgency and complexity of the situation, which are indicators for the appropriateness of Dialogic OD. Touching a *real issue* infuses people with passion and brings the whole system back to life, unleashing blocked energies just by addressing and giving a name to what is, genuinely, a burning question. Passion and vitality are energetic engines, generative forces of novelty and improvement. Touching an *urgent issue* can bring a living system to an intense enough level of energy due to concern or despair, enabling the opening of people's hearts and minds. It makes it more likely people will listen generatively to the emerging future (Scharmer, 2013), willing to experiment with anything that might help (as in 'necessity is the mother of invention'). If we design a process that amplifies this energy, it will probably push the system to self-organize at a higher level of complexity.

2. Client—Is the sponsor/client system ready?

- Is the sponsor/client system *authentically willing* to engage in dialogue over what they care about?

It is enough that they genuinely want it, have the passion to take responsibility and engage in conversation and action. I do not care if they are passionate out of distress, curiosity, or because it is their nature. Their choice gives them agency, a necessary energy for self-organization.

Based on authentic willingness we can proceed with contracting (chap 6) and the first four engagement circles (chaps 5 and 7), working with the client system while building the readiness, relationships, and capacities along the way as needed.

3. Consultant—Is the dialogic practitioner ready?

- Am I available and willing, as an OD practitioner, to engage in working with this system?
- Do I have what they need?
- Can we establish a constructive partnership? Does this system align with my basic values?

If the answers are 'yes'—I continue. If the answers are 'no', depending on the situation, I will either politely counsel my way out of the situation or state my concerns and dialogue about it. The dialogue may result in saying 'yes' to this engagement or pointing the client to other possibilities.

Let us run through this initial screening process again but this time with the initial call that started a 6-month process with 'NTech':

In the first phone call initiated by the HR manager (caller) I explored: "Why are you looking for a consultant?" "Why now?" "How did you reach me?" I learned that NTech was a ten-year-old start-up with 420 employees in the high-tech industry, run by two founding leaders. They were looking for a consultant to help redesign their organizational structure for growth, and I was one of the consultants they were considering. She told me my name was introduced by two managers (not the founders) who had worked with me in the past.

In the first and second meetings with the senior leaders (sponsors, CEO and CFO), I explored: "Why are you looking for a consultant?" "Why now?" "How urgent is it?" "Did you work with consultants before? Tell me about the experience." I learned that NTech was in its 10th year of operation and was economically sound and had a very good reputation, but was not yet profitable. I had the impression they were highly professional and virtuous people. They had engaged in the process of finding a consultant for about a year. The way they framed their need and burning question was, "We need an organizational structure. The company is too big to keep on managing everyone by ourselves."

Feeling a little confused I asked, "You say this is urgent, and I can absolutely see why. At the same time, I'm puzzled that it is taking a year to find an appropriate consultant." They responded that "the situation is very complicated. Everyone feels they work for us personally. We don't want people to feel insulted or demoted." As I was listening, I was sensing both deep care for the people, but also financial prudence and ambivalence. I knew I had to challenge a little more both the perceived urgency of the situation, their commitment to change, and their ability to consider the personal changes it may require from them.

They had used a consultant previously and had a good experience. To the question "why me?" They had a surprising answer. "We heard that you will not give up on us and will not give in to us." I must admit I liked it both for the accuracy of how I work and for the freedom and legitimacy to bring those parts of me to the assignment.

After gathering the initial information and impressions and discussing it with the client, I took the time and space alone, as I always do, to ask myself three essential assessment questions of pre-entry to know if I sense that there are minimal conditions to proceed:

Is the situation ready/suitable?

Our assessment was that the situation was complex, with real burning issues and a few interrelated challenges. They had to stop directly managing 420 people, they had not been profitable in ten years, and planning major growth is always a complex situation. The founders' age added to the sense of urgency. They wanted to find successors in the next few years. They did not have any easy answers or ready-made solutions.

Is the client system ready?

I found an authentic willingness to inquire and dialogue. The sponsors readily took responsibility to engage in conversation and take action. Their devotion to employees made a participatory process the natural choice. After the founders reflected on their personal possibilities and committed to a timeline, I felt more assured about the founders' readiness. It was enough to proceed with contracting and widening engagement.

Is the consultant ready?

I was ready and willing to work with them. I also thought their company and managerial values resonated in a compatible way with mine. What especially made me feel I was ready to work with them was the quality of contact we created and their ability to talk, listen and explore.

Some situations produce a clear-cut triple "yes" of readiness in the initial call or meeting, yet it is often more complicated, as I describe in the Safe case below.

What if the client is not yet ready?

- What happens when the pre-entry readiness assessment is not clear-cut?
- How do we proceed when the client is not ready for dialogic work?

If there is ambivalence or doubt (like in NTech), I offer a mini-contract to explore what is needed and build readiness. This is a short exploratory process of determining together what they need and what process could address it.

Sometimes the consultant and the client make a leap of faith and start the process anyway. If this is the case, it is important to contract in a way that enables real choice-points (see in detail in chapter 6) and build readiness through creating widening circles of engagement. After every circle, it is important to pause to re-evaluate: Do we proceed in the dialogic process or choose differently (chapter 5, 7)?

What if Dialogic OD is not suitable to the client or the situation?

You have a choice:

- Offer more approaches to professional OD work that are within your field of expertise (if you are interested) and discuss suitability.
- Recommend other professionals.
- Just say no.

If there is no match between you and the client, do not take the work. Both of you deserve better.

A colleague and friend of mine introduced me to a brand-new CEO of "Safe" an insurance company. She had worked with this leader before, creating a very successful transformational change in his previous role as a CEO. This time she recommended me since they both thought that a participatory, whole system process would be needed to generate trust and engagement in a system the CEO was new to. The three of us met, and everything seemed promising.

As we met with the wider management circle, and later on a preparatory team, I could feel, in my body, the tension and the inability/fear to be authentic and speak openly. I brought it up with the CEO and he was under the impression that there was openness and that he was very well accepted. My perception was different. I sensed there was 'a secret' that people might be reasonably afraid to talk about (e.g., it may risk their jobs). I asked for a few personal introductory meetings with key figures so they could have a safer environment and found out it was not the CEO they were afraid of; it was the Board of Directors—who fired the previous CEO—they were afraid of. They did not believe any change was possible and believed that speaking the truth may cost them their job.

After gathering the initial information and impressions and talking with the client and my colleague friend, I took the time and space to ask myself the three essential assessment questions of pre-entry:

Is the situation ready/suitable? No, my assessment was that there was no burning question. Moreover, I felt the CEO did not have the power or the legitimate authority to use a dialogic process and let the people participate in leading the organization.

Are the people in the client system ready? No, the sponsor was ready in terms of willingness, but my impression was that he was not reading the more subtle layers of the situation. People lacked an authentic willingness to dialogue. They were in survival mode of careful, obedient participation in what was necessary.

Is the consultant ready? No, I was unwilling to work with the client because it was not a safe enough place for the people or for Organization Development.

I shared my concerns with the CEO and asked him to involve his superiors in the process. He tried to assure me that I was wrong. He was recently hired and believed the Board trusted him and his ability to run the organization independently. I was open and ready to change my mind. It was possible the organizational veterans were wrong, yet my intuition felt sure this was not the case. I must admit that if not for the persuasion of my colleague friend who introduced me to this project I would have left this project much earlier. I slowed down a little to see what would happen. Slowing down was very helpful. A month after the Board of Directors learned about the CEO's plans and understood how different it was from the existing culture of fear and obedience, he was fired.

There was no willingness to engage in any dialogue. The Board of Directors believed they knew all the 'what and how' needed, and wanted an 'executor' as a CEO. Such values and ways of conduct are not compatible with Organization Development.

One clarification about assessment:

Using diagnostic thinking with a dialogic mindset

Diagnostic thinking plays an important part in every assessment by using theory and past experience to create impressions and hypotheses. When doing a readiness assessment, or any other assessment in Dialogic OD, combining a diagnostic with a dialogic mindset ought to be present in more than one way:

- Do not hold your impressions as "this is the truth, let me give you an expert diagnosis," but as "my best understanding up until now is..." Ask questions and do the best you can to keep your mind, heart, and will open.
- Voice your impressions and engage in conversation with the client, discussing assessments and implications. The conversation itself gives valuable information to you and the client as to the ability to develop a dialogic relationship. This is true for the pre-entry process and throughout.
- We notice what we notice mainly because of what we expect to see. We use the diagnostic mindset's models to choose what to pay attention to. You are always working from a model, whether you are aware of it or not. Work at being aware of the models that encase your thinking, and motivate your actions. Be aware of your biases and limitations. Make your models, and improving them, a topic of conversation.
- Do not expect the client to stop using a diagnostic mindset during a generative change process. These are not either/or, both are needed (Hasting & Schwarz, in press). Sometimes "getting the facts" (Diagnostic) is the most useful inquiry, and other times "what do people think and want to co-create?" (Dialogic) is required. These inquiries can go on in parallel, complementing one another. It is our job to work with a dialogic mindset not only when we are working dialogically but also when we are combining both.

Table 2: Threshold for Entry Questions

Screening for Suitability	• How do we know if the client system is ready for dialogic work? • When are the conditions suitable and when are they not?
Initial Assessment With Client system	**Present:** • Why are you looking for assistance? Why now? • What brought you to me? • What is it that is bothering you? What keeps you sleepless at night? • What do you hope from this process? **Past:** • What did you already try and how did it work/didn't work for you? • What are your past experiences in working with consultants? **Future:** • If I had a magic wand and I could promise you an answer to one question only, a critical and essential question that, if answered, will clear the picture for you and the rest will easily follow… what would this question be? • Imagine it worked very well, we are after the intervention process, and you are happy and satisfied with everything—tell me what is making you so happy? What brought us to this point? What has changed?
Screening the 3 C's for Three "yeses" of readiness	1. **Context**—is the situation ready? • Is this an adaptive challenge/wicked problem? • Is there a real burning issue to which no one has a good enough answer? • Is this a situation that calls for a new and unknown path for which there is no straightforward remedy that is available?

Table 2: Threshold for Entry Questions *(continued)*

Screening the 3 C's for Three "yeses" of readiness *(continued)*	2. **Client system**—is the sponsor/client system ready? • Is the sponsor/client system authentically willing to engage in dialogue over what they care about?—(it's a yes) • What happens when the pre-entry readiness assessment is not clear cut?—(slow down for personal work and build readiness) • How do we proceed when the client is willing but not ready for dialogic work? —(leap of faith while enabling choice points and building readiness) 3. **Consultant**—is the practitioner ready? • Am I available and willing, as an OD practitioner, to engage in working with this system? • Do I have what they need? • Can we establish a constructive partnership? Does this system align with my basic values? Sometimes the "yes" is not clear and sometimes it's a "no" • What if Dialogic OD is not suitable to the client or the situation? (Offer other approaches, or other professionals. Also, you can just say no)

When we complete our initial readiness with a triple 'yes'—we continue working with the caller and sponsor to build alignment and a covenant relationship, as described in the next chapter.

FIVE

Caller and Sponsor Circles of Engagement

Entering each new circle in the Swirling Spiral Model will always require some successful resolution of the main task of the previous circle and assessment of readiness for the next circle. As we move from one circle to the next, I will describe what takes place, the main task, challenges and evocative inquiry questions. I will also point to the unique swirl that manifests in this circle and spell out the unique emergent outcomes.

Since each circle assumes a choice point, a decision to be made by both the client system and the consultant, all chapters on practice (chapters 5, 6, 7) will also refer to readiness-building and concurrent assessment that takes place in each circle.

Before we enter

As described in chapter 2, there is some initial work of preparing yourself as a Dialogic OD practitioner that needs to occur before meeting a client. You have probably taken workshops in specific methods like Appreciative Inquiry, World Café, Open Space Technology, Future Search, Art of Hosting, to name a few. They do not, however, necessarily prepare you to embody a dialogic mindset and presence. There are a growing number of OD programs that are taking a dialogic orientation. Joining one of them, locally or internationally, could be helpful to build some foundation of knowledge, awareness, presence and skill.

Getting started with a client implies you have some basic knowledge of Dialogic OD theory, mindset embodiment, and practice. It also implies you have colleagues, perhaps a community of practice and/or a mentor—an experienced dialogic practitioner—to help you when needed. Most experienced OD consultants learned by diving into water above their heads and swimming as well as they could. Start with the way you are now, and do the additional work needed as you proceed. As Aristotle mused in the moto of this chapter: "The things we have to learn before we do them, we learn by doing them".

Aligning with the Caller –The First Circle of Entry

The first person we encounter is usually the caller, the person who calls us to assist the organization. Sometimes the caller has a passion for a specific methodology, and sometimes a general notion that engaging people or using a generative process is needed. In the initial call we learn about the organization, its needs and expectations as stated by the caller (the **purpose**). During the call, we screen for possibilities, listen for needs, see if there are any 'givens' (non-negotiable conditions; Williams, 2007) regarding dates or budget and discuss the motivations and expectations of the caller. We also listen for matches with our competencies, preferences, and general availability as consultants. Find out why the caller contacted you, professionally and personally. Learn together what pains and hopes the client's system carries right now and what they expect from the consultant and the OD process. This is true for both internal and external consultants. This information will serve as guidance: stop if there is no match, or move to the next step. During this time you want to be in **beginner's mind** while listening, questioning and being in dialogic **authentic presence**, describing what is going on in your mind. Try to build an authentically aligned relationship (**covenant relationship**) with the caller as you assess together whether there is pre-entry readiness (chapter 4).

Sometimes the caller is someone who has been given a task to put together a list of potential consultants for a sponsor. S/he has no particular interest in you or the task and will probably ask you to provide written materials or references of some kind. If this is the case, you need them to let/help you meet the actual sponsor(s) as quickly as possible.

Given the caller's potential role throughout the process, a caller who really cares and is engaged becomes a great partner. That person will serve as a bridge and gateway to the new and emerging process and ideas. The caller may represent faith in the consultant, in a certain methodology and/or in dialogic mindset. When the caller is a trusted figure their trust in you and in a dialogic mindset eases the entering and contracting process enormously by creating a leap of faith—also known as 'positive transference' in therapy—transferring the trust the sponsor feels in the caller, to you. This is particularly important in situations where you are unfamiliar to the sponsors, and when the dialogic process is new and possibly disruptive and anxiety-provoking to those in the organization. A trusted caller enables and eases the way to bonding with the dialogic practitioner.

Here's an example of an effective caller...:

> Harriet was a trusted external consultant working with INN, a telecom organization in severe crisis. In 2000, after the dot com bubble burst, the telecom market was dead worldwide, and the worried leadership asked Harriet to find a creative marketing consultant to help them generate sales. She took some time to think and said, "if the market is dead, a marketing specialist will not be helpful. We need a specialist to help us align as an operating system so we survive these tough times and be fast and running to take it when the first opening emerges." Harriet suggested using Open Space Technology as an emergent process for finding a way forward and quickly aligning the whole organization. As a caller, she served as a connector and matchmaker as she knew and appreciated the organization, me, and the methodology. She was a co-consultant, a bridge, and an ally through the three-month process, in each of the entry circles in the spiral, supporting implementation once my contract was over.

This is an example of both the bridge and shortcut a trusted caller can provide. She also brought a profound organizational understanding of the organization and its true needs. Additionally, Harriet offered a suitable process to meet those needs.

Often the caller is our natural and faithful ally. Other times the caller serves only as a gateway performing an administrative function. This relationship with the caller can develop into one of four scenarios:

1. The caller becomes co-owner, engaged in a leading role.

2. The caller serves as a matchmaker, simply introducing the sponsor and consultant. In this case the sponsor serves as both sponsor and caller.

3. The caller serves as a blocker, not letting the consultant pass through. Usually, they want a proposal as a written document. If they are a controlling gatekeeper for the organization, the chance of doing dialogic work is very slim.

4. The caller is the sponsor. In this case, the process can become easier, shorter, and even more powerful.

In my career, time and again, it was a passionate caller that created initial conditions in the system to consider emergent, generative, whole system processes. Or a caller that was open enough to let the consultant meet the sponsor in person early in the process, and by doing so, allowed for direct exposure to the dialogic way of being and doing OD.

The caller must be ready to take some risks to suggest the organization embarks on a new adventure. Usually callers carry a sense of huge responsibility and a personal threat. They risk either being rewarded as a savior or being blamed and shunned if the whole thing fails. Hence, we often find that the effective caller is an entrepreneurial type of consultant or manager, an early adopter of new trends, usually with personal power and influence that can hold ground in chaotic situations.

What the caller is going through was beautifully expressed by Shirley, a strategic planner in a regional municipality:

> "After two years in office as the governor of 'Desert Dreams' regional municipality, my boss, the Governor, had completed all his election promises. Other politicians offered the advice, 'just do nothing and get re-elected at the end of the four-year term.' That did not suit him or me, as his strategic planner. Around that time, I took part in a generative change process with 220 people (Averbuch, 2006) and came out of it certain this was the way to go. We could ask our constituencies, the people who elected him and the people we were obligated to serve. It took some effort to persuade the Governor to sponsor such a process, and I took it upon myself as the strategic planner of the regional municipality to make it happen in a couple of months by handling all practicalities. The most difficult thing was the uncertainty, allowing things to

emerge. For example, the moment I am sitting in the basketball stadium, the large event is about to start and I do not have the faintest idea how many people will show up, or whether they will show up at all! The Governor came to me and said, 'Shirley, it is a waste of time; people are not coming.' An hour later—250 people showed up! But I was still very worried: what if no one will engage or initiate topics?! It was not an easy place for a planner who feels responsible for all that."

Six years later, when the Governor decided not to run again, Shirley ran for office and was elected as Governor for two consecutive terms, using dialogic processes with citizens and neighboring regional municipalities.

A caller must be ready to wade through some rough waters and be instrumental as an inside resource when anxieties arise. Be aware of the caller's intentions, risks, and needs. Talk, consult, guide, and support the caller throughout the process. **(covenant relationship).**

Do not confuse anxiety or fear of the process with unwillingness to dialogue or be actively engaged. Anxiety, a need to control, and ego are all part of the journey of dialogic work and are important sources of information (chapter 7). Anxiety and fear need to be acknowledged, discussed and tended to as we go along (**welcoming climate**).

Match or no match choice point

At the caller circle, the consultant and the caller may find there is no match with dialogic processes and separate. The "no match" can happen for budgetary reasons or due to scheduling conflicts. My experience is that whenever alignment existed between the two of us over the nature of the adaptive challenge to be addressed and the suitability of Dialogic OD, the caller insisted on giving it a try and meeting with the sponsor. The caller also insisted on continuing even if time, space or money did not yet match, believing that if it is the right match, all will come into place eventually.

I never agree to produce a proposal without meeting the sponsor. Usually one of us has one or two points to consider. Sometimes when the situation is not straightforward I contract with the caller for one or two meetings with them and the sponsor (could include few relevant others) for examining what is needed and how to formulate the whole process and contract (**evocative inquiry**). Contracting is discussed in more detail in the next chapter.

Caller circle—Transitional questions to next stage:

- Is the caller ready for an emergent process, curious and willing to explore the unknown?

And/or:

- Will the caller enable and support a meeting between sponsor and consultant?

If one of these developmental tasks is accomplished it moves us to the second circle—the sponsor.

Partnering with the Sponsor—the Second Circle of Entry

The Second circle of engagement is with the sponsor. The sponsor is the person/s in charge, with formal power and authority over the relevant organizational system (or with well-accepted leadership if it is a temporary or informal system).

Our initial conversation with the sponsor will preferably take place in a comfortable space and is free from disturbances. In this conversation, we learn about what is bothering the sponsor, what is their image of a desired future **(the purpose)**, expectations from the consultant and from the process, and their perception of their role in it. We listen and we discuss. The consultant is in **beginner's mind** while listening and questioning and in an **authentic dialogic presence** while exploring with the sponsor whether there is pre-entry readiness of the context, client and consultant (3 C's).

Our working process with the sponsor serves as an important beginning experience and a living example of the dialogic mindset and the development of a **covenant relationship**. I come open and attentive for this conversation. I start with pure listening and later use the present-past-future initial screening questions checklist presented in chapter 4. You may also use various ways to focus on the desired future, such as an appreciative interview (Cooperrider, Whitney & Stavros, 2008), or generative questions and imagery (Bushe, 2007).

During this conversation, the consultant and sponsor mutually assess the sponsor's readiness for generative change. The questions we explore together are:

- Is the sponsor open to deeply listen to multiple diverse opinions?
- Is the sponsor willing to let go of attachment to specific prescribed outcomes?
- Will the sponsor encourage experimentation and embrace mistakes as part of exploration?
- Is the sponsor ready to invite engagement and share leadership with a circle of diverse, caring stakeholders?

Throughout the conversation, stay curious about what the sponsor hopes to gain from a Dialogic OD process (or specific methodology). Make sure that they understand what that requires in terms of all points listed above. Confirm they understand the different kinds of engagement and leadership required in a generative change process, and allow time and space to discuss fears and apprehensions. Invite the sponsor to imagine themselves letting go of control and enabling dialogue without giving up their responsibility as a leader. Inquire what they think and feel and what they will need from you.

This circle implies an initial assessment of whether you can work together in a commitment to a purpose and to one another. Find out if the sponsor is willing to treat you—the consultant, other engaged people, and the process—in whatever way you think is required for success. If you are not sure of the sponsor's openness to learning from disconfirming information, describe the experience you are having that is making you question that. See how they respond. Are they curious? Are they willing to explore? Explicitly describe what you need from the sponsor to be able to accept the contract. Do not shy away from making concrete requests from the sponsor, such as holding an attitude of being open and transparent, personally participating in the planning team and giving it authority to co-create processes. Describe what a **covenant relationship** with you may look like as you become road companions, in particular: informing and consulting on anything—personal or organizational—that may impact the change process, returning your calls, etc. Make it as clear as possible that your responsibility is to be in covenant with them, committing to see them and their needs at all times. Invite them to be explicit about their wants and needs with you as well. By discussing it, make the psychological contract between you open, clear, and emerging.

Remember that many sponsors have worked with consultants in a totally different way. They may expect to be able 'to pass on the problem' to you and some trusted assistants or managers. This is how most sponsors do most of their leading—delegating responsibility and expecting routine reports. In western society, most of us are socialized to call on experts, whether plumbers, doctors, or pest control, to fix our problems while we are busy doing something else. In this second circle of entry, it is our responsibility to make sure the sponsor understands that in generative change they will need to be personally engaged throughout the process; their presence cannot be delegated.

The sponsor in a generative change process usually performs several roles:

- Identifying the question/challenge they see as the burning issue with no good answer.
- Stating the initial purpose.
- Inviting the engagement of necessary and relevant stakeholders.
- Creating a **welcoming climate** and space where differences are voiced and heard.
- Providing the resources for the process and the initiatives launched.
- Protecting the change process from other forces and conflicts.
- Supporting, nurturing, amplifying, and embedding initiatives and outcomes in the organization.

In this stage, some sponsors will state their 'non-negotiables' as boundaries: things they will not consider and will not support. This might include referring to specific issues (e.g., "we shall not talk about salaries when talking about employee satisfaction") or specific process dynamics (e.g., "what if they self-organize to take no responsibility, we cannot enable that"). This usually happens due to apprehension and anxiety of not being able to predict and control outcomes while unfamiliar with the dynamics of generative change processes and their course.

Make clear to the sponsor that a generative change process is an emergent one that a sponsor influences greatly by their **presence**, by the power of their **purpose**, by their ability to co-create a **welcoming climate,** attracting the necessary stakeholders into meaningful conversations and by generating an **evocative field of inquiry** in self-organization.

Here are a few important points that can help a sponsor who has never experienced generative change prepare for it.

- No one has full control over what people will say or do. In reality, no one ever has (Stacy, 2015). Explore their experience with control and predictability and results from past planned change approaches.
- Self-organizing is happening all the time in all systems.
- In participatory dialogic processes, we work with the natural forces of self-organization rather than against them.
- Collectives have innate intelligence. When you bring together people who truly care about a common purpose and give them opportunities to interact authentically, they will create a self-organizing and self-correcting collective to accomplish that purpose if we do not try to control them.

I advise sponsors not to be preoccupied with setting non-negotiable boundaries and givens but to come open and see what they can support as it emerges. Sponsors are often relieved to discover the sanity and wisdom of the community and learn that people in the organization will find ways to lead and create resources for pursuing what they are passionate about.

Bear in mind that the transition required of a sponsor is not a trivial one. If possible, a short-term personal consultation process is recommended, or at least a few personal meetings, to establish a **covenant relationship** between consultant and sponsor and to focus on the sponsor's purpose and self-perception as a generative leader (Bushe, 2019). This can anchor and accelerate the wider OD process (**welcoming climate**), and enable and promote the sponsor's ability to welcome surprise without being shaken.

Two examples.

In NTech, the 10-year-old start-up run by two founding leaders first described in chapter 3, it was evident that there was a genuine will and yet ambivalence. I said to the two sponsors, "Before committing to an organization-wide process, I suggest it is a good idea to explore the next stage for you personally, in case during the generative change process you see your jobs are no longer needed in the same way." They looked surprised and quite shocked. I continued, "As you develop a process that will respect and be kind to your people, this is a way to be kind to yourselves and prepare for the personal unknown. You may or may not need it, yet it is essential as preparation." A short-term personal exploration took place with each one of them. With the CFO it was short and easy—he had a dozen ideas to carry out, thriving for free time. With the CEO it took two meetings to imagine a career that felt satisfying: as a board member he would be involved yet not in the front line. After attending to their personal future we could move ahead. The sponsors could be present as more open, calm and free to engage in this complex and challenging situation.

In this case, the sponsors developed personal answers to the following question: "How do I radically open myself and the system to bottom-up influence without feeling the ground is shaking under my feet?" (**Evocative inquiry**). This is not an easy transition, skill, or practice. It is important to appreciate the leap of faith required of the sponsor in interactive and emergent work. Dialogic processes carry risky elements for the sponsors, such as increased personal exposure, challenging authority, and a sense of losing control while still being accountable.

Here is another example of preliminary personal work with the sponsor as a part of building readiness to support and reveal the wider process:

Lili, the long-term and esteemed manager of Municipal Psychological Services in Middletown asked for my assistance in a succession process. "I am tired; I want to pass on the baton," she said. Since we had worked together previously, she jumped past the entry process and asked for a two-day management team retreat. To me, she sounded exhausted, burnt out, and sad. I asked to meet her in person to learn more. In the conversation I had the impression she was initiating action too soon and was quitting as a reaction to disappointment and fatigue. I suggested, "Please, let's take three to six meetings for you to explore where you are after 25 years of managing this place with unprecedented success. We want to discover what is happening and what is possible in the organization, but first, let's get clear about what you really wish for yourself and for this service". I insisted, and eventually she agreed. To our surprise, we learned that she was so exhausted because she was embodying a much deeper fatigue of the whole system. After a long period of terrorist attacks, tending to the people affected by the bombings, the psychologists did not have enough time to tend to themselves, and burnout accumulated. We ended up engaged in a threefold process over a four month period:

1. Short (three meetings) personal process with her for clarification and grounding;

2. A day and a half retreat with management in one of their homes, for clarification and grounding (who are we? where are we now? where do we want to be as a system? what will take us there?);

3. Half a day of system-wide generative conversation to launch a professional self-organizing program for learning and development for next year.

By the end of this process morale was up again, alignment and sense of belonging restored, and they had a relevant learning and development plan they committed to execute. And Lili? She didn't rush out. She took the time for a well-managed succession process. After two years, she handed the baton to her replacement.

In this story the sponsor, who was also the caller, came 'knowing what to do' yet worn out as a person. It is important to hold on and not proceed immediately for two reasons. First—personal—it is highly important both for humanistic and for organizational functioning reasons that we tend to the person in the sponsor's role and really see him or her, understand and nourish what is needed now for healing and grounding (**covenant relationship**). Second—systemic—burnout is taking a toll and people need to be tended to (**welcoming climate**). Only after doing that can we look together at what needs to change, allowing for a shared time of 'not knowing' and exploration (**evocative inquiry**) to inform us so that relevant and valid ideas about what to do next can emerge.

Dialogic OD and generative change are not an ideology. There are times it is more useful and even necessary, and times it is not. The same goes for using large group interventions. I tend to discuss with the sponsor the different possibilities to answer their organizational and personal purpose and needs. When a Dialogic OD practitioner makes use of large group (Bunker & Alban, 2006) and whole system methodologies (Holman, Devane & Cady, 2007) over a critical issue, there are some risks to weigh against the potential rewards. The large number of people and diversity of participants amplify the expectations and visibility of every move. The commitment to transparency, 'truth telling', and shared leadership makes it impossible to cover things up and release information only where and when suitable to the sponsor (as is the norm in controlled processes). This, in turn, increases the sponsor's anxiety over personal exposure and creates a sense of vulnerability. While being open to outcomes, the sponsor and others may be surprised by what is revealed. For example, we may find out there is very little energy and commitment over an issue the sponsor strongly cares about, leaving authority disappointed or 'shamed'. This must be weighed against the high gain potential: rapid transformative change and the creation of a more agile, vital and adaptive organization. Discussing all this with the sponsor is part of your covenant. (**covenant relationship**).

What is important for Generative Leadership?

Intention is a crucial component. The sponsor of generative change must be authentic, open to outcomes, ready to welcome diverse points of view, present and visible in the process. If a sponsor can hold a beginner's mind and a dialogic authentic presence—conversation, creativity and self-organization will follow. If the sponsor is manipulative in asking people to participate in identifying changes that are already decided, it can cost relationships, trust, morale, and the potential for working together in the future. If the commitment is not authentic, the work will backfire. Be sure that the sponsor takes the time and has the space to understand and make a conscious choice out of a few good alternatives—dialogic and others—to address the situation (**welcoming climate and evocative inquiry**).

Assessing the readiness of a sponsor can have a straightforward answer and can also have the following challenges:

- The sponsor uses command and control language but is genuinely open to trying this new way of work, believing it can be suitable for the challenge.

Rule of thumb: If the intention is genuine the readiness and 'new language' will be acquired along the way.

- The sponsor is enthusiastic about generative change but cannot let go of control (sometimes even believing s/he can). Here the potential for failure is high since we run the risk of building trust and collective expectations for real engagement, only to fail when the process reaches a point that the sponsor cannot tolerate any more and they take back control by giving orders. People will feel deceived and betrayed and the process may make things worse than if no OD project had been started.

Rule of thumb: If the sponsor is too enthusiastic and blind to/denies any personal challenges s/he may encounter in this process, observe the way s/he interacts with the management team. Is there an open and challenging dialogue? If not, get suspicious and take more time to prepare the sponsor to be successful. Confront them with the observations that worry you and see if they can engage in dialogue. If you think they are not ready, try to make sure their managers are invited as stakeholders to support the process. If the sponsor's poor judgment or actions occur at a critical moment, there is leadership to witness and help the generative change process unfold successfully.

Special considerations in situations when you are the caller, sponsor and/or host

Sometimes we initiate a dialogic process in our organization or in a community we are part of. In this case, we can be both caller and sponsor, or caller and facilitator or all three all at once.

Being a caller and a sponsor is usually not an issue as long as you are not also the facilitator. Having a consultant who is not the sponsor in the initial stages will serve as a check and balance as demonstrated in this chapter in the story of Lili.

Being a sponsor and a facilitator is a rocky and risky road, especially but not solely for a beginner in dialogic work. Why? First and foremost, the sponsor, and all who are engaged in the process, learn about a dialogic mindset, generative change, and leadership through the relationship in the triangle of sponsor-stakeholders-facilitators/consultants. This learning through experiencing becomes impossible if you simultaneously hold the roles of sponsor and facilitator. Second, if you choose to stick to facilitation, it means that the sponsor is not present throughout the process! If you move back and forth from the sponsorship role to the facilitator's role, it is hard to discuss givens, to voice your opinion as part of the conversation, and at the same time hold the ground, free from agenda, for all diverse voice. Third, a sponsor has a long-term history, intentions, responsibilities, and accountabilities for the system. As a host, the consultant has a temporary role. Sometimes they conflict. Sometimes it is too much anxiety to carry alone. Most of the time it becomes very confusing for the people to co-create with you, as they are carrying specific history and expectations and need to shift gears back and forth.

You can safely serve as caller-sponsor-facilitator role if this is a minor issue with a small group and you are not attached to outcomes. It can be very counterproductive if this is not the case.

Back to the sponsor's circle. Now is the time to find out if the developmental tasks of this circle are accomplished:

Sponsor circle—Transitional questions to next stage:

- Is the sponsor ready to be open to diverse opinions, share leadership, and be engaged in an emergent co-creative process with no attachment to predetermined outcomes?
- Is the sponsor willing to engage in co-working with the consultant (you) in a covenant of committing to a purpose and to one another without shame and blame?

One last note about entering a dialogic process: if and when working as a team of consultants, I strongly recommend they all take part in the entry process to the client system. Often, consultants' dialogue between and among themselves in front of the client, and with the client, becomes an inspiration and role model of what trust, respect and co-creative flow between diverse people may look like.

Table 3: Caller and Sponsor circles

Caller	Inquiry	Readiness questions: present, past, future: • What are your hopes and expectations from this process? • What do you need from a consultant? Why did you refer to me? • Do you have any previous experience with Dialogic OD approaches/ methodologies? • How do you imagine your role in the process? • What are the risks you are taking in this process? • What are your aspirations and apprehensions?
	Transition to next stage *outcomes that indicate completion of developmental task*	• Is the caller ready for emergent process, curious and willing to explore the unknown? And/or: • Will the caller enable and support a meeting between sponsor and consultant?
Sponsor	Inquiry	Readiness questions: present, past, future: • What is the purpose of the process? • What are your hopes and expectations from this process? • What do you need from a consultant? Why did you refer to me? • Do you have any previous experience with Dialogic OD approaches/ methodologies? • How do you imagine your role in the process? • What are the risks you are taking in this process? What are your aspirations and apprehensions?

Table 3: Caller and Sponsor circles *(continued)*

Sponsor *(cont)*	Transition to next stage *outcomes that indicate completion of developmental task*	• Is the sponsor ready to be open to diverse opinions, share leadership and be engaged in an emergent co-creative process with no attachment to predetermined outcomes? • Is the sponsor willing to engage in co-working with the consultant (you) in a bond of committing to a purpose and to one another without shame and blame?

When major issues with the sponsor(s) are resolved, this is usually the point in time where a formal contract for the whole process may be signed. In the next chapter, we shall complete the sponsor circle presenting the contracting process in detail. It guides and demonstrates how we can plan, negotiate and contract in a dialogically embodied way.

SIX

Contracting for Emergent Outcomes

- When you hear the term 'contracting', what comes to mind?
- Think of a contracting process you were happy with and proud of. What enabled that quality of feeling?
- In your experience, what is most challenging for you in contracting for Dialogic OD?

By contracting I mean creating the terms of engagement. I tend to see all conversations with the caller and the sponsor in particular, and with the client system in general, as having three dimensions. Like a DNA with three strings intertwined, these are the three dimensions I see in all intersections throughout the whole process:

- **Readiness**- assessing and building, we never quit doing it;
- **Contracting-** creating and clarifying the terms of engagement, is ever adjusting;
- **Entering/engaging**- meeting, connecting, proceeding, meaning-making, co-creating action toward the shared purpose.

Everything we inquire, clarify and discuss together about shared intention, scope, nature of the process, methodologies, and roles, can also be seen as a process of creating the terms of engagement. This chapter focuses mainly on the contracting process that takes place throughout the first two circles with caller and sponsor (chapter 5). It is usually formalized and signed before moving to the third circle of engagement (management team).

To establish any consulting relationship, we need a suitable and enabling contract (Block, 2011). After offering a general concept and definition of a contract, I will use stories to illustrate the intricacy and unique contracting challenges for emergent Dialogic OD.

A note to those in internal consulting roles. While this chapter is written from the perspective of an external consultant, everything said about the contracting process, apart from the consultant's fee section, applies to any internal practitioner embarking on a dialogic project in their organization.

Contract—a definition and a general concept

A contract is an agreement between two or more parties that governs expectations and behavior in the relationship. It clarifies what is asked for and what is promised by all parties. After negotiating and signing a contract, it becomes a reference to come back to when reality changes dramatically, when any one of the parties feels the contract is not supporting the work and should be altered, or that it has been violated. Many OD consultants conduct the contracting process as a conversation where mutual expectations are stated, discussed and agreed upon. This is usually referred to as the 'psychological contract'. The 'formal contract' is a written document signed by both client and consultant. It includes only parts of what was agreed upon in conversation, usually referring to the context, purpose, stages, deliverables, dates and fees of the work, generated as requirements. Sometimes the client organization has a generic formal contract with their suppliers specifying the organization's requirements and obligations to and from the consultant. Read it and see if any adjustments are needed. Do not assume that if it is an organizational template nothing can be changed. Be assertive in crossing out things in the template you don't agree with. A common one to look for is that the client will own any materials you design or use during the change process.

A consulting contract includes both the psychological and the formal contract parts that, after all, are good only as long as both the client and the consultant want the work.

Essential Challenges of the Dialogic OD Contract

When working from a dialogic stance we are entering with a 'not knowing' mindset, co-creating at the edge of what's unknown. These conditions are necessary for new patterns to emerge but are hard to accept in a culture that values control, and in organizations that measure and reward by predetermined results. While we need a contract that reflects agreed-upon intentions, goals, and work plans with estimated costs, paradoxically, at the same time, the contract also needs to welcome disruption, promote change, and invite emergence. This makes it essential for a dialogic contract to contain and work well with multiple and opposing forces and have the capacity to hold and align creative tensions between opposing poles.

The polarities (contradicting forces that pull in opposite directions) and paradoxes we often meet while contracting for Dialogic OD work are:

- Desire to know in unclear and unpredictable situations
- Measurable results for unknown answers
- Simplicity to meet complexity
- Planned processes that promote emerging patterns
- Predetermined yet choice-full options

In the contracting process we want to meet the challenge of embracing creative tension in a way that turns polarities into opportunities for generativity and creativity.

During the contracting stage, the consultant has maximum leverage and power to negotiate with the client. Use this power to enable and support the work. If you want the work and are afraid to risk it, feel threatened by competition, want to be loved, accepted, and appreciated, you run the risk of disempowering yourself at this crucial beginning. Often, the consultant feels s/he is the one who must pass a test. Remember, it is a mutual test, or a mutual inquiry, of suitability. Like in marriage, it must be good and satisfying for both sides to work well, and in complex and unstable reality—more so.

Contract Basics

Contracts, in general, are composed of the following elements:

1. Purpose
2. Deliverables

3. Roles and expectations
4. Consultant's Fee
5. Boundaries

These five elements are relevant in every OD contracting process (Block, 2011). Let us walk through these elements to discern what is unique and crucial to contract for if we want to enable and support Dialogic OD work.

Purpose

The purpose of the contract is different from the purpose that will power the generative change process. The contract's purpose states the shared intention of the consultant and sponsor(s), and the value we intend to bring and to whom. The overarching purpose of Dialogic OD work is to create conditions for a collective quest, through which a picture of a shared purpose and a picture of a desired future will emerge. Generative conversations between passionate stakeholders will take place and bear new ideas and actions, resulting in a more adaptable and resilient system, more able to achieve its organiztional shared purpose.

A Dialogic OD contract's purpose is articulated in a particular way, different from contracting for the top-down, pre-determined results of planned change. The contract should reflect the following four basic requirements of the dialogic mindset:

1. The basic attitude of **'not knowing'** and inviting collective discovery, which is very different from a 'knowing' and harnessing stance.
2. It prescribes the **engagement of diverse players** in a generative and non-hierarchical mode of decision-making and communication, rather than a top-down hierarchical one.
3. Both the **process and the results are emergent** and co-created. Not only the results are emergent.
4. **Future-focused, with possibility-driven definitions** of what is desired, rather than problem-solving or analyzing what went wrong in the past, assigning blame, or trying to eliminate or fix.

The story of OP illustrates how we **refocus the purpose** with a caller and sponsor in the initial conversation:

> One day I got a phone call inviting me to consider working with a division of a high-tech global company. The caller, from HR, said he was referred to me as a 'motivation specialist'. The stated issue was that now that the market was growing, they were afraid to lose their key employees to other organizations that might offer more attractive compensation. I asked what their vision of a desired future was and I got the impression that they wanted to move from an adversarial relationship to a partnership with their key employees. I told him I am not a 'motivation specialist,' but I can help create favorable conditions for genuine conversation with the people themselves, who are 'the experts' of their own motivation. After few more meetings with the HR person (caller) and the CEO (sponsor), the consultant's defined role moved from providing expert advice to facilitating a dialogic whole system process, in which all employees were invited to participate. Later, the theme shifted as well.

In this story, the client came with a fear, holding an avoidance-driven image of a desired future. A 'key employees will not leave' statement of the adaptive challenge reflected and fed their fear. As I worked with the caller and sponsor to formulate our contract, the description of the adaptive challenge shifted to a possibility-centered image of the future, from fear of leaving to transforming the relationship. We eventually stated the purpose of the contract as follows: 'employees will be proud and happy to belong to the division'. Along with this new definition came the commitment to what it required. They took it upon themselves to become curious and open, inviting non-hierarchical dialogue with whoever chose to engage. They adopted a not-knowing stance, inviting self-organization and calling forth the emergence of new adaptive patterns.

Deliverables

Deliverables are the service/merchandise offered: what is it, by when will it be delivered, and to whom? Since in Dialogic OD, we are working with a *process* that is participatory, self-organizing, co-led, and transparent, deliverables are co-created and emergent. This is a creature with an intricate nature. So what are we contracting for? What are we selling/buying?

I usually identify deliverables in phases of the work plan. Here's an example:

Phase 1: Initial Pathfinding—the deliverable is clarity

- What is the problem or the challenge?
- What is the current image of a desired future?
- Learn about different methodologies that could be the means to get there and decide whether to proceed with the consultant.

Phase 1 is the entry and readiness phase. It is a contract to explore whether Dialogic OD is the path sponsors want to take. A renewed contract will need to be devised by the end of this phase, or the consultant will exit. The following phases are often contracted together, but they are distinct.

Phase 2: Preparing—the deliverables are infrastructures, initial conditions for success, and cultivating a spirit of engaged evocative inquiry.

- Cultivate covenant relationship with caller and sponsor.
- Form a diverse planning team to co-create and co-own the process.
- Articulate the shared purpose that will attract the engagement of stakeholders.
- Construct an invitation and inquiry stated in a generative, compelling way that starts movement toward a desired future.
- Informed and enthusiastic choice of Dialogic OD approach and method(s).
- Creatively engaged diverse stakeholder community.
- Detailed planning for logistics, documentation, after the event support for initiatives, etc.

Phase 2 deliverables are contracted for with the sponsor, as s/he decides to take the dialogic path, with the understanding that the actual process and delivery will be co-created with the planning team of diverse stakeholders. This team includes the caller, sponsor, some management members and a mix of maximum diversity of stakeholders who reflect the whole system.

Phase 3: Facilitating/Hosting Generative Conversations—the deliverables are events that create new conversations where people identify new ideas and actions to accomplish the purpose.

In this phase, we are hosting conversations that matter and creating emergent outcomes that move the organization toward the purpose of the process. The specific deliverables will differ from one purpose to another but all generative processes will probably have, along with specific emergent outcomes, the following eight process outcomes:

- Engagement and a greater sense of community for the individuals involved.
- A better and more visceral understanding of the whole and my part in it.
- Alignment and attunement to what is needed for the future.
- Increased sense of possibility and hope.
- Shedding old patterns and formulating new and more adaptive patterns.
- New ideas, experimentation, and mobilization for action.
- Self-organized groups working towards the purpose.
- Release of vital energy that was previously locked or blocked.

Phase 4: Anchoring and accelerating change—the deliverables here are amplifying desirable outcomes, supporting implementation of emergent outcomes, and embedding them in the organization's culture.

Whenever possible, contract for this stage or work to ensure there are internal resources and people that will be responsible for it. Deliverables may range from:

- Processes for monitoring and ensuring leaders know what is happening with the initiatives that emerged from Phase 3 and know when they need to take action to nurture, amplify and/or embed new structures and processes in the organization.

- Helping leaders identify where current organizational structures and processes need to change to align with the new organizational culture they are creating.
- Information channels and meetings to inform, reflect, share insights and learn from the entire process.

Managing Expectations

The client's assumptions about the nature of OD services often parallels the western-medicine metaphor: you come to the doctor with a problem and the doctor's role is to go through diagnosis and prognosis, develop a treatment plan and implement it. The patient can be passive, compliant, or inquisitive. Bluntly put, it is a battle in which the doctor is your hired gun to kill the disease while you go on with your life.

The OD consultant's metaphor about the nature of OD services is often of a midwife: inviting and helpful in birthing the new, assisting with the course of nature, yet very aware it is not the consultant's child and they are not the ones giving birth. This clash in expectations is challenged in all types of OD but more so in Dialogic OD.

Sponsors have to be more present and engaged throughout the process than they may be used to in other organizational initiatives where they delegate and oversee. It's important that they understand that Dialogic OD is an interactional intervention requiring a different kind of leadership. From the initial stages, their job is to invite, ignite, and share leadership with others. In Senge, Scharmer's and others (2005) terms, they are invited 'to let go in order to let come'. Let go of predetermined ideas and expected results, and let the new order, patterns and ideas, come and emerge from future possibilities. They probably have to stay in a place of not knowing longer than is comfortable for good enough options to appear.

Covenant relations between consultant-client

The covenant type of relationship between consultant and sponsor, as described in the swirling spiral working model (chapter 2) and sponsor's circle (chapter 5), is critical to understanding, and a key to navigating, role expectations. A covenant relationship means we are committing to work together in uncertainty out of a personal choice to commit to a higher cause/shared purpose anchored in values and beliefs. This is a strong bond to a purpose, oneself, and one another as we step together in an unknown future.

Expecting a covenant relationship with the client while negotiating a contract is not conventional, and it is a disruptive expectation. Although many times managers regard this disruption as a pleasant surprise, it takes time to understand that even though we are negotiating we are on the same side, not opposing parties. As consultants our work is to speak openly and honestly of what we know and what we cannot know or promise. While we assure our clients that a generative change process will be more effective for managing an adaptive challenge than traditional top-down methods, nothing is certain when engaging complexity. We educate our clients about this type of contacting 'from the same side' by being it, modeling it and speaking from it at all times. Usually, our client is not used to this type of interaction with consultants during a contracting process. Just talking about covenant relationships to clients is not effective. You have to embody it, be it, to gain the client's trust.

The consultant's expectations of the consulting relationship:

A dialogic partnership consists of engaged and active associates that strive to embody and conduct themselves according to the following principles:

1. free and informed choice at every stage
2. open communication
3. care for the whole system as well as its parts
4. commitment to learn and improve in a welcoming climate
5. radically accepting and appreciating 'what is' as a starting point in the process
6. embracing disruption, welcoming and inviting self-organization and emergence.

Every OD consultant has to decide what they want and what they need from every consulting relationship. Be aware of your own boundaries and favorable conditions and communicate this to the client in clear everyday language. Real bonding and an alliance that comes from authenticity and mutual respect enables the relative safety that is needed to invite the new and unknown into being. These six principles may not characterize the client's culture when you first enter the system, but you have to be clear that cultivating these principles in their actions creates the conditions for success.

Consultant's Fees

When the outcomes are unknown, and the content and the structure of the process of work are emergent, how do you contract for your fee? A story of my early days illuminates some of these challenges:

> In the year 2000, when I was just beginning my Dialogic OD practice, a military organization was looking for a participatory planning process for the year 2020. The sponsor was impressed with Open Space Technology and felt they had found the participatory methodology they desired. My business partner and I were thrilled to be asked to do the work. We soon discovered that we did not have the slightest idea how to contract for our fee.
>
> As we struggled to describe and budget the work process we encountered two problems:
>
> 1. The client wanted to know precisely what the process would look like and its total cost.
>
> 2. The budget seemed to have too many hours and be too costly.
>
> The client system did not have the patience to cultivate the conditions and ripeness for an emergent process. It became clear that if we charged by the hour, we were doomed. The client would choose minimal preparation, regardless of what we felt was necessary. Charging by the hour meant we risked putting ourselves in an adversarial, instead of a covenant relationship, with the client.
>
> We decided to offer the client system a choice between an hourly rate and a fixed price. We preferred the fixed price approach since we

> wanted the liberty to exercise our uncompromised commitment to quality. We said, "Throughout the engagement, we will urge you to do all that is needed to create conditions for the success of this process." By working in a fixed-price mode we took the financial risk upon ourselves so that every hour we spent was taken from our own pocket. This created the trust and alignment between client and consultant systems to generate our partnership.

One of our challenges was to align our interests. Another challenge was to create congruence between our dialogic mindset of supporting emergence and the client's choice in every step while meeting our need, as consultants, to make a living. The story continues:

> We believe that the client's decision-making must be conscious and choice-full at all times. We did much of the entry process and built a planning team before there was a signed contract. Only after investing 50 hours of work for a project of 200 hours, we asked, "Do we proceed? Are you ready to commit to creating suitable conditions for the process?" We made it absolutely possible and legitimate that they could choose not to proceed. Luckily they did.
>
> During the next six months, we worked dozens of hours with other organizations, helping them articulate their purpose, educating them about different dialogic possibilities and presenting methodologies, only to recommend that they should not work with us. We found out it was not a way to make a living!

It took a few months of sitting in this unrest to see that the initial process with the client was not pre-sales. We were doing a short-term OD consultation focused on initial pathfinding. We could sell it as a mini-project for developing clarity concerning their main challenge, articulating purpose, creating a picture of desired future, and learning about the variety of approaches to get there. We concluded that for the dialogic stance to be genuine, partnership needs to be sustainable both for the client and consultant. This part should be compensated.

Like most consultants, we were used to charging by the day or by the hour. In our dialogic practice we developed a fixed-rate compensation model I encourage you to bring into your practice. The fixed price is, by far, my preferred model when working with an emergent dialogic process. A pre-determined fixed rate best aligns all interests, enables a covenant relationship and supports collective, emergent work. The consultant can show up whenever and wherever they want without the client worrying that the money-meter is running. People other than the sponsor can ask the consultant for help without needing pre-approval or a budget. The consultant doesn't feel like s/he is pushed to show they are providing value in every minute—they can take the time to listen deeply, supporting participants in owning and co-creating the emergent process and outcomes. An additional benefit of fixed price is that it requires the client and consultant to be clear from the beginning how they will know the work is finished, providing the clients a sense of control over expenses.

In this model, the client purchases a full process with clear phases and deliverables. Normally they pay a part of the fee at the beginning and then payouts at different milestones. If in one of the initial circles of work, with sponsor or planning team, consultants and client decide to walk away, the consultant is compensated for the invested hours according to a predetermined rate. Another possibility is treating phase 1, the initial pathfinding, as a separate project with an hourly or daily rate. The rest of the project has its own fixed price.

Sometimes bureaucratic rules in an organization make it impossible to offer a fixed price. Then I suggest agreeing to be paid for your time, doubling the fee for large group work because you have to clear the day before to prepare by emptying and tuning yourself and the day after the work requires time to reflect, recover and recharge. This is also the explanation I give the clients.

Boundaries and saying 'no'

Every contract can be violated. Every contract can be terminated. That is part of life. Our duty is to bring a dialogic mindset to the contracting processes and regard it as an opportunity to learn. All parties involved can begin, alter, and end their agreements using OD values and practices. In this nebulous zone where the personal and professional meet, where personal needs and expectations are laid bare, we can manifest the best of who we are. We can be a powerful lesson, of embodying dialogic presence and of deep commitment to the values of a generative process, by staying in the contract and not giving in to lesser conditions than necessary. By negotiating for more authenticity and truth in the relationship and the process, or by walking away and terminating the contract, if essential values are violated.

Some of the important questions in the process of contracting have to do with its termination. When do you walk out of a Dialogic OD contract? Why? How? I have confronted these questions quite a few times. This is a story of a time I was ready to walk away.

> At INN, the organization that desperately needed to make "one million this year", everything was prepared in a Dialogic OD spirit. A few days before the whole system's gathering, the CEO approached me with a grim face and said: "We are bleeding. We need to lay off another 100 people before the end of the month, but I am not going to say anything until after the event because it will ruin everything".
>
> I was confused, shocked and angry. I started explaining to the CEO and the HR manager why it was critically important to be transparent and truthful in our intention, communication and conduct. For some long minutes I felt, for the first time in this process that it was me against them. Eventually I said, "I do not have an idea how we should tell them and exactly when but I know there is no way for me to facilitate this event without them knowing the real situation." I knew this was a boundary I would not cross.
>
> The dialogue between us continued as we were engaged in finding the proper way. On the day of the event, the CEO opened the gathering with an announcement, " I would rather promise there will be no more layoffs, but this is not possible. We do not know who yet, but 100 more people will have to leave the organization in the near future. We decided not to postpone the gathering since the organization is bleeding and every day counts in the collective effort to turn back to vitality." These words were magical in their impact. They signaled the authenticity and the kind of relationship the leadership wanted to have with its employees. We started our work together, holding this difficult reality with courage, responsibility and grace. It supported the work of creating a community that could weather this storm.

Now that the psychological and formal contract is in place, we can work with the next two engagement circles.

SEVEN

Management Team and Planning Team Circles of Engagement

The first two entry circles of Caller and Sponsor established a strong enough foundation and a decision, backed by a formal and psychological contract, to take the next step.

Engaging with the Management Team —The third circle of Entry

The management group usually runs the organization—or their part of it—with the sponsor, and is used to being in charge. This group also carries responsibility and accountability for organizational outcomes and may thus feel anxious about letting processes develop bottom-up while sharing leadership with diverse stakeholders (planning team). Since people look to their managers for clues to figure out what is expected of them, management members critically influence the process.

While most of the management team do not have a sponsorship role, they have a natural and vital influence. Usually, some or all management members are involved, directly or as backstage advisors, in the exploration and/or decision-making process with the sponsor before formal contracting. If the burning issue is related directly to one of the management member's scope of responsibility, that person has to be in the exploration and decision-making circle with the sponsor and given the opportunity to share sponsorship with the senior leader. When the process is on a limited scale and affects just a part of the organization, the sponsor of the process will preferably be the head of that area, get the senior leader's blessing, and invite him/her and others to actively participate as stakeholders.

Assuming the sponsor made the decision to continue with a dialogic process in the previous circle, how do we enter this third circle of the management as a team? Management members can be enthusiastic toward the dialogic process, or they can object and reject it. Objecting and rejecting usually indicates they don't believe this could work for the benefit of the organization. Or they are anxious about losing control over processes they are accountable for. Engaging with the management team as a group, informing and listening, attending to the wisdom of their suggestions and apprehensions, getting a buy-in/embrace of the dialogic process, and starting to co-create the diverse planning team—is the third circle.

To begin, I like to meet the management as a team and provide all the information they need about Dialogic OD and generative change processes. This may include stories, demonstrations, referrals, and a short workshop to enable direct experience with a specific methodology or Dialogic OD. I enter this circle with a lot of respect for the responsibility that lies on their shoulders and compassion for their needs and worries when choosing a process. The nature of our conversation upon entry resembles the way I work with the caller and sponsor or, in fact, anyone. I do not sell the process or try to persuade it is the right one. I do not promise what I cannot control. I always listen, offer information and share my experience, feelings and thoughts as needed. Management is the first place that I insist they 'try it on for themselves as a group'. I use one or two dialogic methodologies in a short demonstration so that the caller, sponsor and management members can have a first-hand experience, a taste, of how it may actually feel. The demonstration can be about a real issue that management is struggling with, about the overarching theme/question for the process that the caller, sponsor and I discussed in the previous circles, or about them and their role in the process. Here is an example of choosing a theme that suits both the situation and the methodology I am demonstrating:

> With the management team at OP, I demonstrated Open Space Technology with the following question: *'what are my/our issues and challenges in this Dialogic OD process?'* We opened an hour-long space, they created

an agenda, and people self-organized into conversations. After the demonstration I invited everyone to debrief their experiences, being open to every question and concern. I was not 'answering' but rather 'staying with' what emerged as management members sorted out their thoughts and emotions. The sponsor told what he went through when looking for a process to meet the organizational challenge and shared his thoughts, hopes and aspirations. I invited management members' perceptions of the burning issues and desired future (chapter 4), and any givens (time, dates, locations, budget). We explored if a Dialogic OD approach made sense and discussed what was needed for transition to a dialogic leadership mindset and action. Once the group felt comfortable that this was the way to go, we moved to mapping stakeholders of the change process and discussed creating a planning team that reflects this whole.

During the management team meetings, the sponsor, caller and I cultivate a **welcoming climate** for everyone to be in authentic presence, expressing what they think and feel as a contribution to the emergent process. We invite all of us to be open to listen and be changed by listening. Developing these norms is the core of dialogic spirit, and usually this is when a management group embraces the dialogic process. If not, we listen and adjust as described later in the case stories. The third circle of engagement is a process of psychologically contracting with the management by exploring, doubting, sharing, experimenting and refining.

Do not be tempted to skip meeting with the management team as a group. Be respectful, helpful and compassionate to the disruption experienced by managers embarking on a dialogic process. In an emergent dialogic process, communication and inquiry are often decentralized, and yet management stays responsible and accountable for organizational outcomes. This is quite a challenge since Dialogic OD flattens the hierarchy by opening channels of conversation and treating all who are invited as equals. During whole system's gatherings (generative events), all stakeholders are perceived as holding different yet valuable perspectives of the whole that need to be present and heard.

Generative events can be viewed and structured as temporary moments, a 'transitional space' for playing in a way that is free for spontaneity and emergence (Winnicott, 2005). They can be treated as 'cultural islands' where new norms and rules that violate and suspend existing culture promote dialogue and learning (Bennis & Schein, 1965). All participants know that when the event is over, the hierarchy returns. This can be tremendously valuable for generating breakthrough ideas and insights and as a space to explore a visceral sense of a new way of being and doing in collectives, a new culture.

Yet, for more culturally transformative purposes, when leaders want to create more engaged, adaptive, agile organizations, the intent is that the day-to-day status quo will change as well. If the intention from the start is for cultural change, the dialogic culture ought to be encouraged and legitimized by managers between and after events, setting expectations for everyone to speak up and interact with anyone they care to. That implies creating a welcoming attitude for everyone to express and initiate anything they are passionate about regardless of rank and expertise. This can be confusing and threatening for people holding formal authority.

Conversations about management's role, and the thoughts and feelings of managers, are invited, addressed, and tended to. Coping with the challenge of giving up some of their control and authority, we may direct managers' attention to the possibilities that open for them in this process: the bounty of new ideas, enthusiasm, and partnership with motivated individuals.

Here is a story of a self-managed unit of four people. Though they are part of a large organization, they are totally independent. They can be looked at both as management and as core members of the planning team of their change process (Averbuch, 2013). This story illustrates the dynamics of people with the power to execute who need to give some of their power away to transform the system they are part of.

> I was called with the following request; help this unit orient itself strategically, in a short and affordable process, to gain a clear focus and become a central player in their educational field. The caller, who was also the sponsor, asked for my assistance, knowing he wanted a dialogic process with many stakeholders, hoping to disrupt the exiting culture and assist the department in moving from a defensive-survival mode to a proactive one.
>
> After a fruitful meeting with the sponsor, I met the entire unit's staff and learned they were clear on why they wanted a consultant and their

goals. The question was: how? It seemed clear to me that inviting all their stakeholders, working transparently to learn the actors and actions in their local field, discussing the unique virtues, threats and opportunities of this unit, and initiating strategic alliances with other stakeholders, was the way to go. But were they ready for that kind of a process?

The challenge was to help them see the opportunity in using massive stakeholder participation with their small team of four, who were quite skeptical of using self-organizing and emergent processes in a large group.

They expressed three fears:

1. A "fear of drowning" in the process, afraid to lose control over their work.

2. A "fear of alienation", afraid that the process will point in directions they are not interested in or do not know how to do.

3. A "fear of abandonment", afraid that stakeholders will not come, and if they do, they'll never stay the whole day.

There were a few thresholds to cross in entering this circle. The enthusiastic sponsor that brought me was a new manager for them and had a very different attitude. He was open and adventurous while they were more cautious. They had spent five years struggling for the unit's survival by independently creating their own resources in a poorly managed organization. While they shared an intention to create a strategy for the unit, the swirl from authentic presence to emergent outcomes was yet to be generated.

The sponsor and I made it clear that they would choose the process they felt comfortable with. My role was to present possibilities, inform, listen and help design a process where they had enough control yet left enough room for something new to emerge. Being assured they had a choice created a **welcoming climate** amongst all. Without giving it a name or a label, they gradually opened up to possibilities as they experienced a **covenant relationship**, a commitment both to the cause and to them as people. When we all came to this, **authentically, evocative inquiry** of what was suitable and what was possible unfolded naturally.

Working with this group taught me two important lessons about the fears of people in charge and how to work with them:

Respect fears and listen to their guidance. As I listened to their concerns, I moved from perceiving the three fears as 'resistance to change' to 'valuable information'. We let their fears guide us in co-creating a wiser generative change process: a combination of highly managed and structured ways of data gathering, new directions and alliance creation, with a loosely managed, emergent, process of meaning-making. We created a two-day stakeholder process with a week in between each day. This gave them a sense of control because we could learn and correct as we went (and we did).

Working step by step with 'what is', created readiness for the next step. The initial skepticism changed into expressed fear. By listening to the fear and letting it inform us, we walked together, building trust and courage, ownership and co-leadership. A few additional factors created readiness for the next steps: experiencing the dialogic mindset with me and with their manager, getting an enthusiastic 'yes' when inviting external stakeholders, getting appreciation from other players in the field, collecting more information through phone interviews, and planning, integrating and thinking together.

This story illustrates that if the consultant and sponsor work together, embodying dialogic processes and presence, ready to be changed by dialogue, it can be enough to prepare for working dialogically with management and the larger stakeholder community.

Management circle—Transitional question to next stage:

- Are senior managers ready to see other people, who share the same reality, as equally important and travel companions?
- Are people in power ready to take a risk by temporarily giving up some of their power, in the hope of gaining a wider view and a more adaptive pattern of coping?

Whenever I enter the management circle of engagement with curiosity and empathy, the answer to these questions is 'Yes'. Plus, the psychological contract with the sponsor expands to include the management team. If there is no work with management, or if an initial negative attitude is taken as 'resistance to change', not as 'information to work with', it can backfire. An enthusiastic sponsor is not enough.

Co-owning with The Planning Team—the fourth circle of Entry

There are many different names for the diverse group of people that carry the dialogic process forward: 'design team', 'planning team', 'preparatory team', and 'steering committee' are common. The planning team of a dialogic change process is the first circle that did not exist before the process started. The way I work, the planning team is an authorized body set up to support a Dialogic OD process. Their task may range from serving as a sounding board for the sponsor and consultant (seldom—if this is the case, 'preparatory team' reflects their role better) to serving as co-creators and co-owners (often) of the whole process from scratch. In that case, 'planning team/steering committee' reflects it well. I always try to use a name that does not carry negative connotations in the specific organization. If needed, I make one up.

While creating the planning team, we must remember that this is a circle that we initiate and facilitate, unlike the previous circles. We have a leadership role in forming it and in generating and protecting the conditions for success. Planning teams I work with include the sponsor, caller, Dialogic OD practitioner (one, or more, if we work as a team of consultants), internal change agents if there are any, some senior managers who choose to, and a mix of maximum diversity (in age, sex, location, rank, role, expertise, etc.) of people who choose to engage in this role.

There are two key factors in this entry circle: the planning team members genuinely <u>choose</u> this engagement and—the planning team <u>reflects</u> the diversity of the stakeholders. Three main reasons why:

1. By reflecting the whole system, the planning team can more easily create a full picture of the whole system and adaptive challenge from firsthand knowledge. Chances are high that what is important to the whole will show up in a diverse planning team.
2. As a microcosm, the planning team is where the organization first learns how to be and work in dialogic ways. This creates ripple effects by carrying this knowledge into the organization in many formal and informal ways.
3. If properly structured, the planning team will include everyone needed to make wise decisions in a short time.

It is worth putting in the effort to make sure the committee is diverse enough.

What do you do if you find, upon your entry, there already is a 'planning team' for the process? First, you take the time to listen and learn how they see their role, purpose and leadership, and then you inform and educate about the nature of planning teams needed for dialogic processes.

Since, in a Dialogic OD process, the planning team is a reflection of the whole system, we start with asking the question, "Who is missing? Who else should we invite if we want to fully reflect the relevant stakeholders and the diversity of the system in this team?" As team members start inviting, just keep on asking yourselves 'who is missing?' and keep adding until it reflects the whole (Averbuch, 2006).

Creating a planning team

Make sure the sponsor and the caller understand they are vital and essential members of the planning team. Then, with these two and the management team, create a map of relevant stakeholders.

Whom to invite?

Think of the stakeholders that compose the 'whole system' (Weisbord & Janoff, 2000), people who must change or will be affected by the change to accomplish the purpose. Also bring diversity in: race, seniority (newcomers and veterans), gender, age, geography, profession, attitude (including passionate opponents; skeptics), etc. When the team starts meeting, keep asking "who is missing?" throughout the whole process. Invite and add people as necessary.

How to invite?

I usually recommend a combination of the following two approaches for inviting people to a planning team. These two approaches, with some adjustments, repeat themselves as a means of inviting the 'whole system', the fifth circle of engagement.

1. **Specific invitation**: we invite the sponsor, caller and management to think of specific people whom they feel 'must be' in the planning team because they have one or more of the characteristics below:

- Passion to take responsibility for creating the path for others.
- Talents, skills, connections, or a personality that are valuable gifts to the work.
- Caring and concern for the current state.

The sponsor, caller, or the management team are advised to make a personal invitation—preferably an informal or semiformal conversation—that will leave the person feeling invited and appreciated and yet with a genuine choice on whether or not to join. It is an invitation that communicates 'everyone is invited but no one has to accept' (Owen, 1997).

2. **General invitation**: The sponsor announces the process to take place in the organization and extends an invitation to anyone who cares to influence the nature of the process to join the planning team. People interested in taking responsibility, who are ready and willing to invest the time and energy, will show up.

A note: when we have a large number of people volunteering for the planning team we can choose to work with all of them, or we may ask some to be a core team and others to serve as a sounding board if there is a question the planning team wants to take to a larger group.

What is the planning team's work?

The role of planning teams, and the work of creating and working with them, are covered in detail in the BMI Series book by Sarah Lewis (2021). Here I will just briefly outline my thoughts.

The planning team is the riverbed for the change process, and its role is to own the process and co-lead it. In more practical language, it usually means to:

1. Clarify the **purpose** of the process, its intentions and aspirations.
2. Formulate the **focal theme/question**(s) of inquiry reflecting the purpose.
3. Choose the **methodology** and approve the **design** of the process.
4. **Create conditions for success.**

If the process includes one or more large group gatherings, the planning team is responsible for event preparations. This is covered in detail in the BMI Series book by Mark McKergow (2020). The basic decisions the team must make are:

- **Scope**: Who will take part? How long? Where? When?
- **Invitation**: How to invite? What approaches to use for promoting the process?
- **Hosting**: Logistics, hospitable space, food and extracurricular activities.
- **Documentation and communication**: Gathering the information, capturing meaning, insights, ideas, and initiatives, being transparent about what will happen with this information.
- **Sustainability**: Planning for 'the day after', for sustaining and amplifying change
    - What will be done with the products of the process?
    - Who and how will initiatives be supported and desired changes nurtured?

A tip for planning teams during events:

I invite every participant of the event to join the 'evening meeting of the planning team'. This open boundary of the planning team serves the process in several ways:

- enhancing energy flow and people's choice
- being enriched by diverse collective wisdom and engagement
- debriefing and digesting today's impressions
- adjusting the next day's planning
- deepening relationships through direct engagement

This happens to be one of the most effective fluid structures I have used. In a collegial dialogic spirit, we all share feelings and thoughts of the day, connect, digest, and recalibrate ourselves and the emergent process. Surprisingly it also serves some of the participants as a takeaway of a compact, semiformal way to engage and co-create across hierarchy on any planning issue.

Everything created by the planning team is presented transparently, in writing and/or as announcements at the beginning of any large group gathering, building trust in the wider field and enabling people to make informed choices about navigating in this self-organizing field of opportunities.

The Planning team is where the contract for dialogue becomes a shared reality

This circle of entry is where psychological contracting is most intense, in three complementary aspects:

1. Planning team meetings are used, consciously and unconsciously, to sense and test the genuine intentions of the sponsor and management team about sharing power, leadership and partnership with non-management members.
2. Testing whether they can trust the consultant both professionally (does s/he know what s/he is doing?) and personally (is s/he trustworthy? will s/he see us, care for us and be true to dialogic values as presented?). A challenging part in this contracting is that the consultant is both in an expert role (of dialogic methodologies and process) and in a facilitative role. Sometimes, to ease the potential conflict, I use two chairs that I move between; one represents the 'expert' role, and the other represents the 'process consultant' role.
3. The planning team also serves as the experimental ground for testing, validating and refining ideas generated and contracted for in previous circles (methodology, purpose, etc.), and ideas generated by the planning team. Here is where the theoretical contracting becomes a living shared reality.

The planning team meetings enable essential exploration and confrontations between parts of the system that are ordinarily foreign, suspicious or blind to one another. Team meetings facilitated by the consultant helps members have a 'first-hand' experience of Dialogic OD that hopefully increases their enthusiasm and allows them to embody the process as they spread the word and invite others to join in. Through this work, team members build skills for inviting in a dialogic spirit and cultivating covenant relationship.

A **covenant relationship** amongst all who participate in this process is established through shared ownership and work. A covenant relationship is a conduit of the spirit, builder of infrastructure and creator of conditions necessary for the success of the Dialogic OD process.

The following story illustrates how this new psychological contract is created. The planning team challenges the sponsor and designs a process that enables open communication resulting in trust:

> In OP, a high-tech organization, there was a palpable issue of distrust following a major downsizing. The sponsors wanted me to help retain their people. The planning team formulated the theme, "How can we make our division a place that we are proud and happy to belong"? The planning team also wanted to make sure no one would be hurt as a result of speaking up. They challenged the CEO many times: 'what if people say things you do not like? What if they initiate actions you do not care for?' They were unwilling to proceed until they were convinced he was sincere in his intention and conduct, creating a new and different psychological contract of trust and collaboration. After they were sufficiently convinced, they created a presentation. They delivered it, in face-to-face meetings, to everyone in the organization, presenting the process and its opportunities in groups of 20-70 employees at a time. They met all 750 employees, insisting every committee member will only present to people who do not report to them directly so people felt free to ask questions and say what they really thought and felt.

This story shows how a psychological contract gets developed through the actions people take. Norms get established during entry.

Planning teams not only challenge the sponsor but also challenge the facilitator to see if s/he only talks about 'every voice is important and decision making is emergent', or if s/he generates this reality in the room. Here's one of my favorite examples:

> Dan, the finance vice president (VP) of OP, was an active planning team member. While planning the two-day retreat, the sleeping logistics in the hotel were raised. Most of the committee's members, myself included, thought that a night together would deepen the process. The finance VP spoke decisively: "I say we sleep at home." Something in the way he spoke communicated, 'I am the senior manager in this room and you

have to comply'. I felt sick in my body, attacked and shut down. I knew that was the feeling in the room. Knowing this was a point of transition I turned to him and asked: "please tell me who is speaking: is it your opinion as a person that you would rather sleep at home than share a room in a hotel? Or is it from your finance role, something you want to say about the budget? Are there any 'givens'?" He smiled and said that he, as an individual, really hates sleeping with a roommate and that he, as Finance VP, thought it wasn't possible because there wasn't a budget to put each person in a separate room. I asked him to tell us what the budget was and then turned to everyone saying, "In a Dialogic OD process Dan can tell us the budget as the Finance VP, but the decision whether to sleep in a hotel or not is the team's decision." There was silence in the room and I felt all the eyes on me as if I was committing suicide. I continued, "If the planning team feels it is vital for the process that people stay together overnight, we can try to think about solutions that stay within the budget, such as two, or even more people in a room sponsored by the organization, allowing for whoever wants to personally pay for a single room." There was a breath, and I could feel myself energetically embraced with gratitude by the planning team members for 'bravery in speaking up'. That was uncommon until then and more common from that incident on.

To perform their role well, planning teams usually go through two common shifts:

1. **A shift from being 'representatives' to being 'members' of a group that reflects the whole.** If each one is dared to be authentically and fully themselves—not there to represent others—that is enough.
2. **A shift in inclination from separating boundaries to permeable boundaries.** A planning team can start with excluding subgroups ('they are against us'; 'they are too difficult to handle'...) and gradually open to inviting people they do not normally consider as part of their organization. People such as clients, end-users, regulators, strategic allies, or even competitors. As they work together in dialogue, they realize the wonders of diversity and want more of it (Averbuch 2006).

We generate the contract as a living reality by being the change we want to bring. I urge the planning team to hold everything we do as 'our evolving draft of today', making it easier to build on other people's ideas and constantly improve as we hold a collective **evocative field of inquiry** and execution.

If the dialogic process of building a planning team is successful, more initiative and self-organization will emerge. Leadership will be shared by many, and we shall witness everyone providing their best ideas, information, assessments and advice about what is happening and what should be done over different issues as needed.

Planning team circle—Transitional question to next stage:

- Is the planning team owning the process? Are they engaged in inviting others, co-leading with a dialogic spirit and co-managing the conditions for success?

Table 4: Management and Planning Team Circles

Management	Inquiry	**Readiness questions: present and past, with emphasis on Future:** • Do you have any previous experience with Dialogic OD approaches/methodologies? • How do you imagine your role in the process? • What are your hopes, fears and aspirations? • What is the purpose of the process?
	Transition to next stage *outcomes that indicate completion of developmental task*	• Are senior managers ready to see other people, who share the same reality, as equally important and travel companions? • Are people in power ready to take a risk by temporarily giving up some of their power, in the hope of gaining a wider view and a more adaptive pattern of coping?

Table 4: Management and Planning Team circles *(continued)*

Planning team The planning team is the first circle that did not exist before the process started	Forming Inquiry	• Who to invite? (whole system and ecosystem, affecting and affected by the change) • How to invite? (specific and general invitations of relevant people) • What brought you to this team? What is your passion? **Readiness questions: present and past, with emphasis on Future:** • Do you have any previous experience with Dialogic OD approaches/methodologies? • What are your aspirations and apprehensions? • Who is missing? (ongoing question) • What is the updated shared purpose/ inviting question? • What process do we choose and how do we create the conditions for success?
	Transition to next state *outcomes that indicate completion of developmental task*	• Is the planning team owning the process? Are they engaged in inviting others, co-leading with a dialogic spirit and co-managing the conditions for success?

This spiral sequence of the circles of entry and engagement described in chapters 5, 6, and 7, is a pattern you will encounter again and again, tailored to every new organizational challenge. The repetition, the owned experience, the constant reflection and the ripples it creates offer a dialogic way of being and doing in an organizational life.

Beginning Today—a concluding note

Just do it!—Introducing Dialogic OD to your existing clients by using mini processes

As this book is ending and you may be on the threshold of a new beginning, I want to add to your possibilities of experimenting by sharing some very simple ways of introducing dialogic mini-processes in any organization that knows you. You begin by asking yourself:

- Where can I change one simple element to make it more dialogic?

If you come with the dialogic mindset and embody it as your way of working, **you do not have to call it any name or say anything special. Just do it.** Experiment with changing at least one element in a habitual structure with a playful, open attitude. Here are four general ideas as starters:

1. Take any real issue that needs to be discussed and offer to facilitate it with a dialogic mindset.
2. Add a diverse team to plan annual ceremonies or routine organizational events.
3. Open existing weekly (periodical) meetings by making the name and

theme of the meeting transparent to the organization and inviting diversity as a limited number of approved self-selected guests.

4. Treat participants and clients as colleagues in co-creation. Periodically consult with them openly.

On the other side of this spectrum of engaging and experimenting with dialogue and participation, I have a heartfelt warning: For anyone fascinated with dialogic work, **do not fall into the missionary trap and become a preacher and advocate** for a dialogic stance and methodologies as an ideology. Holding a dialogic stance as an ideology means you come from 'knowing better', and prescribe how to be. That is wrapping a diagnostic mindset in a dialogic facade. Remember: dialogue is a philosophy and not an ideology. Make it part of your practice to experiment with new possibilities, knowing that by definition, in a dialogic stance, we always have only temporary and partial understanding.

Just be it!—Cultivating Authentic Presence and Beginner's mind

Becoming a Dialogic OD practitioner means holding the mindset and skills of both professional knowledge and performance, and having the beginner's mind and presence of an artistic improviser. We have to embody Dialogic OD knowledge and paradoxically forget it, at least to an extent, while we listen deeply and innocently to the moment: open, curious, ready, and playful—in beginner's mind.

Presence and mindset are the cornerstones to the depth of your practice. To what extent do you show up as you are? Are you committed to being true to yourself, others and emergent reality? Are you willing to be authentic and vulnerable with courage and consistency? How do you embrace and manage turbulent emotions as they arise?

Cultivating presence

Many people and schools of thought offer paths to being an authentic presence. For me, Angeles Arrien's (1993) 'four fold way' was and still is a precious guide. Arrien, a sociologist and anthropologist, draws from indigenous wisdom four archetypical ways of creating a life worth living, which perfectly describes the mature dialogic practitioner:

Show up and choose to be present	The way of the warrior
Pay attention to what has heart and meaning	The way of the healer
Tell the truth without blame or judgment	The way of the visionary
Be open to outcome, not attached to outcome	The way of the teacher

Walking these archetypical paths will root you in who you really are, both personally and collectively. Arrien's book can serve you both to explore who you are and to develop a fuller courageous and authentic presence.

Cultivating Beginner's Mind

- What brings you joy?
- What triggers the inner permission to be playful and silly?

Is it young children that you are fond of? Is it singing? Dancing? Improvising? All of these can serve as means to cultivate beginner's mind. Discover what works for you.

In cultivating beginner's mind, we are pretty much unlearning and shedding inhibitions and restrictions. Allowing ourselves to act from the internal freedom of a loved, inquisitive, one-year-old and yet keep the professional and role responsibility. We need a community of practice to deepen into this fully.

These practices can be helpful for finding companions:

- Belong generatively: Belong to people, groups, communities, and places that appreciate you for who you are and bring out the best in you. Do not try 'to fit in' places where that is not so.
- Bond in a way that facilitates your becoming the best of who you can be.
- Bond with people through shared higher intentions and create covenant relationships with them, where committing to one another is always in the context of a larger ecosystem and intention

for a better future for one and all. Develop shared philosophies, clarify principles, and create emerging fields of possibility together.

For professional development as practitioners, we need our own networks, groups, and fields for belonging. Communities of practice, strategic alliances, online communities, learning cohorts, and circles of friends who offer camaraderie, collaborative learning, support, and co-creation.

Can you think of a community of practice or courses that cultivate this type of presence, mindset and belonging?

A concluding note

Thank you for staying in conversation until now. Time to end and depart. Time for concluding and making room for new beginnings.

Please lean back and take a moment to reflect:

- What is your most important take-away from this book?
- What surprised you?
- What closed for you? What opened?
- What are your feelings and thoughts at this crossroad?
- What do you feel the urge to experiment with?

If you get a hold of a vibrant life thread in you—follow it. Call, offer, experiment, and when you are done, do it again. And again. Remembering Aristotle's wisdom: "*The things we have to learn before we do them, we learn by doing them…*" (Aristotle. The Nicomachean Ethics)

This conversation is over, yet the door stays open to continue the personal-professional dialogue. I would be happy to hear your curiosities and learnings. You can find me at www.tovaaverbuch.com or at tova.averbuch@gmail.com.

References

Arrien, A. (1993). *The four fold way: Walking the paths of the warrior, teacher, healer, and visionary.* HarperCollins.

Averbuch, T. (2006). Building coalitions to create a community planning tool in Israel. In B. Bunker, & B. Alban (Eds.). *The handbook of large group methods* (pp.219-230). Jossey-Bass.

Averbuch, T. (2011). Opening space for collective wisdom. Lecture given at TEDx Jaffa. https://www.youtube.com/watch?v=adf1sjnXERE&ab_channel=TEDxTalks

Averbuch, T. (2013). The little engine that could. *Challenging organizations and society, reflective hybrids, 2*(2). Retrieved from http://www.cos-journal.com/2013-volume-2-issue-2/.

Averbuch T. (2015). Entering, readiness and contracting for dialogic OD. In G. R. Bushe, & R. J. Marshak (Eds.), *Dialogic organization development (pp. 219-244)*. Berrett-Koehler.

Bennis, W.G. & Schein, E.G. (Eds.) (1965). *Personal and organizational change through group methods.* Wiley.

Block, P. (2011). *Flawless consulting: A guide to getting your expertise used* (3rd Ed.). Wiley-Pfeiffer.

Brown, B. (2012). *Daring greatly*. Penguin.

Buber, M. (1970). *I and thou.* Charles Scribner's Sons.

Bunker, B., & Alban, B. (Eds.) (2006). The handbook of large group methods. Jossey-Bass.

Bushe, G.R. (2007). Appreciative Inquiry is not (just) about the positive. *Organization Development Practitioner, 39*(4), 30-35.

Bushe, G.R. (2009). *Clear leadership*, (Rev Ed.). Davies-Black.

Bushe, G.R. (2019) Generative leadership. *Canadian Journal of Physician Leadership*, *5*(3), 141-147.

Bushe, G.R. (2020). *The dynamics of generative change.* BMI Publishing.

Bushe, G.R., & Marshak, R.J. (Eds.) (2015). *Dialogic organization development: The theory and practice of transformational change.* Berrett-Koehler.

Carse, J.P. (1986). *Finite and infinite games: A vision of life as play and possibility.* Free Press.

Cooperrider, D.L., Whitney, D., & Stavros, J. (2008). *Appreciative inquiry handbook*. Crown.

Driver, T.F. (1991). *The magic of ritual: Our need for liberating rites that transform our lives and communities.* Harper Collins.

Gendlin, E. T. (2007). *Focusing.* Bantam Dell.

Hasting, B.J., & Schwarz, G.M. (in press). Leading change processes for success: A dynamic application of diagnostic and dialogic organization development. *Journal of Applied Behavioral Science*. May, 2021. doi/10.1177/00218863211019561.

Heifetz R., & Laurie, D. (1997). The work of leadership. *Harvard Business Review, 75*(1), 124-134.
Holman, P., Devane, T., & Cady, S. (Eds.) (2007). *The change handbook.* Berrett-Koehler.
Holman, P. (2015). Complexity, self-organization and emergence. In G. R. Bushe, & R. J. Marshak (Eds.), *Dialogic organization development (pp. 123-150).* Berrett-Koehler.
Human, L.J., Sandstrom, G.M., Biesanz, J.C. & Dunn, E.W. (2013). Accurate first impressions leave a lasting impression. *Social Psychological & Personality Science, 4*(4), 395–402.
Janoff, S. (2021). Striving for wholeness: It is time for social scientists to make a loud noise. In J.M. Bartunek (Ed.). *Social scientists confronting global crises.* Routledge.
Lewis, S. (2021). *Co-creating planning teams for dialogic OD.* BMI Publishing.
McKergow, M. (2020). *Hosting generative change.* BMI Publishing.
Owen, H. (1997). *Open space technology: A user's guide.* Berrett-Koehler.
Rutter, M. (2002). Nature, nurture, and development: From evangelism through science toward policy and practice. *Child Development, 73*(1), 1–21.
Senge, P., Scharmer, O., Jaworski, J., & Flowers, B.S. (2005). *Presence.* S.O.L.
Scharmer, O. (2013). *Leading from the emerging future.* Berrett-Koehler.
Schein, E. (1988). *Process consultation (Rev. Ed.).* Addison-Wesley.
Schein, E. (2009). *Helping.* Berrett-Koehler.
Schein, E. (2021*). Humble inquiry.* Berrett-Koehler.
Shaw, P. (2002). *Changing conversations in organizations: A complexity approach to change.* Routledge.
Sinek, S. (2019). *The infinite game.* Portfolio/Penguin.
Snowden, D. J., & Boone, M. E. (2007). A leader's framework for decision-making. *Harvard Business Review, 85*(11), 69–76.
Stacey, R. (2015). Understanding organizations as complex responsive processes of relating. In G.R. Bushe & R.J. Marshak (Eds.). *Dialogic organization development* (pp. 151-175). Berrett-Koehler.
Suzuki, S. (1995). *Zen mind, beginner's mind.* Weatherhill.
Weisbord, M., & Janoff, S. (2000). *Future search* (2nd Ed.). Berrett-Koehler.
Williams, B. (2007.) The genuine contact program. In P. Holman, T. Devane, & S. Cady (Eds.). *The change handbook (2nd ed., pp.227-233).* Berrett-Koehler.
Winnicott, W. (2005). *Playing and reality.* Routledge.

Printed in Great Britain
by Amazon

37451399R00066